THE INCOMPLETE ADULT

CONTRIBUTIONS IN SOCIOLOGY

Series Editor: Don Martindale

Capitalists Without Capitalism: The Jains of India and the Quakers of the West
Balwant Nevaskar

Black Belonging: A Study of the Social Correlates of Work Relations Among Negroes
Jack C. Ross and Raymond H. Wheeler

The School Managers: Power and Conflict in American Public Education
Donald J. McCarty and Charles E. Ramsey

The Social Dimensions of Mental Illness, Alcoholism, and Drug Dependence
Don Martindale and Edith Martindale

Those People: The Subculture of a Housing Project
Colette Pétonnet. Rita Smidt, Translator

Sociology in Israel
Leonard Weller

The Revolutionary Party: Essays in the Sociology of Politics
Feliks Gross

Group Interaction as Therapy: The Use of the Small Group in Corrections
Richard M. Stephenson and Frank R. Scarpitti

Sociology of the Black Experience
Daniel C. Thompson

THE INCOMPLETE ADULT

Social Class Constraints on Personality Development

Margaret J. Lundberg

Contributions in Sociology, Number 15

GREENWOOD PRESS

WESTPORT, CONNECTICUT ● LONDON, ENGLAND

Library of Congress Cataloging in Publication Data

Lundberg, Margaret J
    The incomplete adult   245p. c1974

  (Contributions in sociology, no. 15)
  Bibliography: p. 215-228.
  1. Personality. 2. Social classes. 3. Socialization. I. Title. [DNLM: 1. Personality development.
2. Social class. BF698.9.C8 L962i]
BF698.L8   155.2'34   74-67
ISBN 0-8371-7362-0

Library of Congress Catalog Card Number: 74-67
ISBN: 0-8371-7362-0
First published in 1974

Greenwood Press, a division of Williamhouse-Regency Inc.
51 Riverside Avenue, Westport, Connecticut 06880

Manufactured in the United States of America

11/20/75 - $12.50

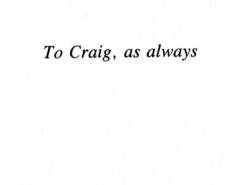

To Craig, as always

Contents

List of Tables

List of Figures

List of Figures

Preface

A period in which it is fashionable and often politic to hold the WASPish middle class responsible for most of the ills of society is not the best time for an impartial study of social class differences in personality development. Nevertheless, the mounting evidence of a systematic, positive relationship between the child's personality development and his social class position cannot be ignored. Both the rate at which the child progresses toward psychological maturity and the ultimate level of development he reaches seem to be strongly affected by his particular social class subculture. The overall conclusion derived from the behavioral science literature is that the chances of achieving full personality development increase with each step increase in social class position.

The corollary—that lower class people typically develop more slowly and less completely than middle class people—will, I fear, raise the hackles of many readers. Some, out of genuine solicitude for the feelings of the poor, are categorically opposed to what they call invidious comparisons between classes. It would be interesting to know how much data has been buried as a result of this attitude. (One apparent example appears in footnote 46 of Chapter 3.) Others, moved less by solicitude for the have-nots than by resentment against the haves, hold that the lower class subculture is superior to that of the middle class—more natural, more spontaneous, for example—and so must produce better personalities. These readers will find it necessary to deny the entire body of evidence cited here in order to protect their position. Still others, viewing the lower class as a perennial threat to their way of life, will be delighted initially to see its personality types unflatteringly described. But their delight will turn into umbrage when they realize that the forces shaping personality prove to be aspects of the subcultural milieu. Not only does this provide the lower class person with an excuse for his "bad" behavior—at the same time it undercuts the middle class person's pride of personal achievement.

As if all this irritation were not enough, I have had the temerity to come up with a happy ending, which of course will affront the prophets of doom. To them I can only say that I, too, was a dedicated pessimist until the logic of the material changed my position. Scholarship is like a mystery ride: though you don't know where it's headed, you can't resist going along. I hope that those readers with rising blood pressure will control it enough to go along with me, even if only to look at the scenery.

The route is straight and simple. In the first chapter we look at the major social classes and their distinctive value systems, then at psychological maturity and the developmental track leading up to it. The emphasis in each case is on discovering what is generally agreed upon as the central tendency. Stripped to their skeletons, the factors reveal basic correspondences pointing to a systematic relationship between social class and maturity level in the three classes dealt with. The next three chapters seek to show how this comes about—by what cognitive, affective, and associational processes membership in a particular social class can stunt or stimulate the development of personality. The fifth chapter presents the outcomes of these processes in terms of adult personality types, and the final one discusses the implications and applications of what may be called the personality dimension of social class.

Whatever his political leaning, the fair-minded reader will agree that a relationship supported by evidence from so many different areas deserves at the very least further study. Besides its intrinsic interest, its potential applications reach into every sphere of social life. And added to these is an ethical purpose on which we can all agree: finding and pulling down the roadblocks to psychological maturity for people of every social level.

THE INCOMPLETE ADULT

1

What We Are Dealing With

Social Class
and
Personality Development

At first glance no two concepts seem farther apart than social class and personality development. One refers to the broadest kind of social structure and the other to the creation of individuality. They are reconciled by the facts that at any given moment every social class is composed of individuals, but that despite their differences these individuals have many ideas and experiences in common. Their personality similarities arise from these common ideas and experiences, that is, from their having been cultured in the same medium. Their differences grow out of choice and chance.

When one considers the almost incredible variation of choice and chance possible in daily life at every level of our society, the wonder is that any group stability or continuity exists. Yet sociology can show that certain social classes have persisted for centuries in spite of constantly changing membership and social conditions, and psychology has demonstrated that the vast array of individual personalities can be meaningfully classified into a small number of types. Both generalizations have been achieved by focusing on similarities rather than on differences.

In searching out the functional relationship between social class and personality development we shall adopt the same strategy and concentrate on central tendencies rather than on variations.[1] Let's begin by identifying those social classes most generally agreed upon and determining what appears to be the main line of personality development.

SOCIAL CLASS: THE MEDIUM AND THE MESSAGE

Like the rest of sociology, the study of social class or stratification is in the natural history stage of scientific development. Its emphasis is still upon such activities as counting, describing and classifying, and the statistical and substantive problems that these involve.[2] The few theories of stratification that have appeared have been of little direct help to investigators attempting to describe the American social class system.

Thrown back on their own resources, field workers have had to content themselves with operational definitions of social class and the consequent limitations on their conclusions. Lack of agreement on the indicators of social class position has in turn led to lack of agreement on the social class boundaries, so that students of stratification have often resembled the blind men trying to describe the elephant. How much of this groping has been due to conservative bias is a matter of opinion; certainly its influence cannot be denied. Apparently until rather recently the desire to believe in the American Dream and to avoid the appearance of Marxist leanings has discouraged the investigation of economic and political roadblocks to upward mobility.[3] Another factor is operative here, too, one which arouses a more sympathetic reaction than ideological bias does. This is the problem of the intercorrelation of indicators.

Faced with the obvious overlapping of income, occupation, education, residential area, status ratings, and consumption patterns, field workers have had only two possible directions in which to move: 1) the compiling of more or less elaborate indices of weighted factors[4] or 2) reliance upon the single indicator thought to cast the widest net.

After more than a quarter-century of operationalizing, we are still without a definitive description of the American stratification system as a whole, but the slow, unpretentious natural history approach is beginning to pay off. The accretion of knowledge about various strata in the system has built up certain points of contrast between strata and certain commonalities within strata. Where the commonalities end and the contrasts begin there are shadowy areas rather than clear-cut lines of demarcation. Yet even in this troublesome question of locating class boundaries several important points of agreement have emerged. And when the findings of studies using different criteria of social class position and different kinds of samples over a twenty-five- or thirty-year period show convergence, their points of agreement must be granted a fair degree of validity and reliability.

The Major Criterion and Resulting Social Class Divisions

Marx regarded the social class system as the inevitable outgrowth of the social organization of work in industrial society. Further, he saw that occupational status largely determines social status, and so he must be credited with identifying the primary criterion used to rank individuals and statuses in a social class system: occupation. Weber might broaden the sociological perspective on stratification by suggesting related criteria, and Warner's use of status alone might make the "reputational method" popular for a time, but evidence has continued to pile up that the significance of these other criteria derives in large part from their overlap with occupation. Warner himself found that

occupation had the highest correlation with his Evaluated Participation Scale.[5] And after a factor analysis made in 1955 of nineteen
different social class indices used in earlier studies, Kahl and
Davis concluded that occupation was the best single indicator of
social class position.[6]

Perhaps the best evidence of the importance of occupation is the
fact that the most generally agreed upon social class division is one
based upon type of occupation. This is the split between manual
and non-manual work or blue-collar versus white-collar. Mayer
calls it "the major class division in the United States."[7] Bronfenbrenner refers to it as the "lowest common denominator" in
stratification studies made before 1958.[8] Blau calls it "a major
class boundary,"[9] and Hamilton "the major line of class
cleavage."[10] Even social class categories which are *not* based
directly upon occupation show the same blue-collar/white-collar
dividing line as the categorization based upon occupation alone.
Compare three of the best known sets of social class categories
with the Edwards occupational categories used in the Census
(Table 1). Centers used subjective class placement as his measuring device, Warner used status ascription by community residents,
and Hollingshead used a modified Edwards scale combined with
residential and educational criteria. Centers found that to those
identifying themselves as such, working class meant the same
thing as is indicated by the Edwards Scale, [11] and lower class
meant being poor and lacking education.[12] Nearly three-quarters
of Centers' business, professional, and white-collar workers identified themselves as upper or middle class, and 79 percent of all
manual workers identified themselves as working or lower class.[13]
    The logical justifications for making the manual/non-manual
break the major class dividing line have been variously stated.
Kohn's explanation is that:

1 Middle class occupations involve the manipulation of inter-

TABLE 1

The Blue-Collar/White-Collar Line in Four Sets of Social Class Categories

Edwards[1]	Centers[2]	Warner[3]	Hollingshead-Redlich[4]
Professional	Upper Class	Upper-Upper Class	Class I
Managerial		Lower-Upper Class	Class II
Clerical	Middle Class	Upper-Middle Class	Class III
Sales		Lower-Middle Class	
Craftsmen, Foremen	Working Class	Upper-Lower Class	Class IV
Operatives			
Service	Lower Class	Lower-Lower Class	Class V
Farm Laborers			
Laborers			

[1] Joseph A. Kahl, *The American Class Structure* (New York: Rinehart, 1957), pp. 64-9.
[2] Richard Centers, *The Psychology of Social Classes* (Princeton, N.J.: Princeton University Press, 1949), p. 77.
[3] W. Lloyd Warner and Paul S. Lunt, *The Social Life of a Modern Community* (New Haven: Yale University Press, 1941), I, p. 85.
[4] August Hollingshead and Frederick C. Redlich, *Social Class and Mental Illness* (New York: Wiley & Sons, 1958), pp. 390-7.

personal relations, ideas, and symbols, while working class occupations involve primarily the manipulation of physical objects.

2 Middle class occupations are more likely to permit self-direction, while working class occupations are more subject to standardization and direct supervision.

3 Getting ahead in middle class occupations is more dependent upon one's own actions, while in working class occupations it is more dependent upon collective action, particularly in unionized industries.[14]

Lipset and Bendix justify this class boundary on statistically based grounds:

1 white-collar jobs usually offer a better future in terms of income than blue-collar jobs;

2 white-collar jobs usually offer higher prestige than blue-collar jobs;

3 white-collar jobs usually require more formal education than blue-collar jobs;

4 white-collar workers, even the lowest paid ones, are more likely than blue-collar workers to think of themselves as middle class and to act out middle class roles in their consumption patterns;

5 white-collar workers, even of the lowest level, are more likely to have political attitudes resembling those of the upper middle class than those of the working class.[15]

They further point out that most white-collar jobs which are anomalous in terms of social class, i.e., lower in income and prestige than some skilled blue-collar jobs, are held by women.

For a few years Warner and his followers made some use of the notion "level of the common man," which obliterated the white-collar/blue-collar line.[16] The term was used in order to emphasize the similarities between the "Lower Middle" and "Upper Lower" classes as compared to the classes on either side, and as such it may have been the precursor of the "Middle America" and "silent majority" notions. The similarities between the two classes, however, were probably due to Warner's choice of reputation and social participation patterns as the criteria of social class and to his omission of the crucial variable, occupation. Because of this the occupational structures of his Lower Middle and Upper Lower classes overlapped, so that each had about the same proportion of skilled and semi-skilled workers. Judging from independent studies using occupation as the criterion of social class, the similarities of Warner's Lower Middle and Upper Lower people in avoiding voluntary associations, in types of organizations joined, in religious involvement, in media behavior, in style of life, and so on are best explained by this overlapping of occupations. Warner himself had found that the non-manual and manual occupational groups were referred to as "the classes" and "the masses" respectively, at least by middle class people.[17] The fact that this distinction existed in the community argues that a significant social boundary had been established, one which was ignored by the "common man" categorization.

The second major point of agreement which emerges from stratification studies of the past few decades is that below the stable blue-collar class is another stratum of blue-collar people with few if any occupational skills and a high rate of unemployment. Mayer considers that this line between "the aristocracy of skilled labor" and "the bulk of semiskilled and unskilled manual" workers is of high sociological significance.[18] Centers established the subjective identity of separate working and lower classes over twenty years ago,[19] and community studies using objective criteria have found at least two subdivisions within the blue-collar category.[20] Yet it was not until the publication of Harrington's *The Other America*[21] in 1962 that investigators felt it necessary to distinguish clearly between these two groups. Even today no standard

nomenclature has been established, and the reader must refer to the
description of the sampling process to determine what a writer
means by "working class" or "lower class." Frequently one of
these terms is used to refer to a combination of the two, a "non-
middle-class" category. For certain limited purposes this lumping
of categories may serve. For the broader purpose of understanding
the stratification system and its effects upon behavior, the differences between the two blue-collar groups must not be lost sight of.

In terms of numbers alone the lowest class would seem to
deserve special attention. Using Walter Miller's figure of 15
percent of the total population,[22] it would number over 27 million.
This is comparable to Myers and Roberts' figure of 18 percent for
New Haven.[23] S. M. Miller, reviewing five outstanding works
which used an economic rather than a life-style criterion like
Walter Miller's, found that "They show remarkable agreement,
despite their different procedures, in estimating that one-quarter to
one-fifth of the United States' population lives below the poverty
line."[24] By this estimate the lower class would number somewhere between 36 and 45 million people. Harrington puts the
figure at 40 to 50 million.[25]

When these people are lumped with the working class group, the
implication is that over 50 percent of the population[26] is relatively
homogeneous. This is patently ridiculous when every piece of
information about them indicates that these two groups are anything but alike. In occupational skill, income or education—the
three most popular objective criteria of social class—the lower
class falls short of the working class on each count. Neither are
they homogeneous in terms of life style, power or prestige. One
has only to compare such exemplars as the restaurant dishwasher
with the factory toolmaker to see this. In the next section we shall
see that the working and lower class groups are more similar to
each other in value orientations than they are to the middle class,
but this is only to repeat again that the basic class cleavage line is
that between the white-collar and blue-collar groups. It does not

mean that the distinction between the working and lower classes should be glossed over or ignored.

Actually, with the government's discovery of "the other America" and the money which has been made available to study it, the lower class has become in the last ten years a prestigious area of investigation and something of a professional specialty. The spate of enthusiasm with which the lower class category is now embraced is evident in the statement that "the line that divides stably-employed, well-educated, well-paid workers from the lower class is becoming more important than the split between upper working class and lower middle class,"[27] and in the return to the notion of a "middle mass," Warner's old "level of the common man."

The racial consciousness of the period has confused the issues somewhat, but evidence is beginning to accumulate which strongly supports the view that social class is a more predictive variable than race. Child-rearing studies of black mothers, for example, show social class differences of the same sort as those found among white mothers.[28] And an important study comparing the significance of race and social class in the same group of disadvantaged children points up the distortion which would occur if black families were unthinkingly assumed to be a subculturally homogeneous group.[29] A summary of these findings is shown in Table 2. Here the level of significance is higher for social class than for race in nine out of the eleven tests, indicating that in these areas social class is the more powerful predictor of behavior. Gans suggests that the same conclusion may be drawn about the relative predictive power of social class and ethnicity.[30] And Kohn and Schooler go even farther by stating that they found class-related orientations to be constant "regardless of race, religion, national background, region of the country and size of community."[31] The fundamental importance of social class could hardly be more strongly underlined.

The convergences which we have found portray the American

TABLE 2
Race and Social Class as Separate Factors

	Significance Levels of Chi Square Tests of Association	
	Black-White	Social Class Level
A. Father present in the home	.01	.001
B. Dilapidated housing	.02	.001
C. Parental educational aspirations for child (Blacks' are higher)	.01	.001
D. Parent's choice of child's future occupation (Blacks' are higher in each social class)	.01	.001
E. Child's own occupational aspiration (Blacks' are higher in each social class)	.02	.005
F. Parental perception of own status in society as improving	.001	.01
G. Crowding in the household	n.s.	.001
H. Occupational mobility of wage-earner	n.s.	.05
I. Nutritional adequacy of child's breakfast	n.s.	.01
J. Mother's presence with child at breakfast (Blacks less often)	.01	n.s.
K. Parental estimation of child's reading ability (Blacks' are less adequate)	.05	n.s.

SOURCE: Richard D. Bloom, Martin Whiteman, and Martin Deutsch, "Race and Social Class as Separate Factors," in Martin Deutsch and Associates, *The Disadvantaged Child* (New York: Basic Books, Inc., 1967), p. 316.

social class structure as being composed of at least three readily identifiable strata: a lower class, a working class, and an extensive middle class. Although everyone recognizes significant differences within the middle class between such groups as are represented by, say, the department store clerk and the doctor or engineer, there is no general agreement as to how or where to draw boundary lines. In speaking of the "amorphous middle classes" Williams says that their subdivisions have "low social visibility."[32] Because they are largely ignored in empirical investigations, we are forced to do without them and therefore to court the danger of over-generalizing about the middle class.

Another amorphous stratum is the upper class, which everyone recognizes as existing somewhere up there but which no one does anything about. At this altitude the criterion of occupation fails us since so many members of the upper class do not work for a living. Education is equally undependable for the same reason, and the usefulness of income is clouded by the qualifying factor of prestige. Clearly a well thought out index will be needed to classify a group which includes both the "jet set" and the "power elite." There are also practical problems such as how to get an adequate sample of these well protected people and how to secure frank answers to questions whose answers would be newsworthy simply because of the respondents' identity. No wonder we know so little about the group at the top of the flagpole. Not only does the upper class per se go unstudied, but it is also generally omitted from studies using social class as a variable. Practically none of the studies cited in this book involved upper class respondents, and so our field is delimited to the three classes already described.

The Social Class Value Systems

Social class position affects personality development by providing differential learning experiences, which for any given class consist of its distinctive value system and interaction patterns, or its subculture. Verbalized values are evidence of ideals and intentions, while interaction patterns may be regarded as values in operation. Obviously both types of indicators are important: what people say and what they do. In the lists of social class values or subcultural themes that follow, it can be seen that interaction patterns are included both implicitly and explicitly.

In his well-known statement of the "publicly dominant" American values, Williams stops short of labeling them middle class values[33] though he sees them as emerging from "the middle-class society of nineteenth-century America."[34] Our own position is that these are properly regarded as middle class values because it is middle class people who tend to live by them, acting them out as well as advocating them. They have become the dominant values of our society partly through the prestige of the middle class and partly through the fact of middle-class control over the educational establishment. Thus blue-collar people become very familiar with them and pay lip service to them or even hold them as ideals. Their everyday interactions, however, are much more likely to be guided by the values of their own social class, which Williams calls "alternative themes" in the context of society as a whole.[35] In his formulation, which follows, the dominant or middle class values are directly compared with these alternative themes, the "rather than's." Number 2 contains the only "rather than" which does not seem to represent a working class value.

1 "American culture is organized around the attempt at active mastery rather than passive acceptance."
2 "Its genius is manipulative rather than contemplative."
3 "Its world-view tends to be open rather than closed: it emphasizes change, flux, movement. . . ."
4 Its primary faith is in rationalism rather than in traditionalism, and it is strongly oriented toward the future.

5 It prefers orderliness to an "unsystematic *ad hoc* acceptance of transitory experience."

6 "With conspicuous deviations, a main theme is a universalistic rather than a particularistic ethic."

7 It stresses equality rather than hierarchy, peer-relations rather than superordinate-subordinate relations.

8 Wherever possible it "emphasizes individual personality rather than group identity and responsibility."[36]

The next two sets of values, which are labelled working class, support the suggestion that Williams' comparison is between middle class and working class values. The first set was drawn up by Miller and Riessman.

1 A striving for stability and security, both at work and at home. This brings about a reluctance to do anything that might disrupt family or peer group security.

2 Traditionalism, deriving from patriarchal extended families with sharply separated sex roles.

3 Intensity. "Many of their attitudes are related to their traditional orientation and they are held unquestioningly in the usual traditional manner."

4 Person-centeredness. The importance of personal qualities and of informal, comfortable relations with people is stressed.

5 Pragmatism and anti-intellectualism. Working class people believe it is results that count. They like the clear action and the understood result and dislike wordy or abstract discussion.

6 Excitement. This theme is often in contradiction to the "traditional" theme. It is held by some subgroups within the working class, notably by adolescent boys and by young unmarried men.[37]

Hoggart's listing of typical British working class values[38] is included here because of its interesting similarity to those of the American working class.

1 An oral and local tradition. Dependence on old sayings, myths, and superstition. Each separate activity has its own folklore.[39] "To live in the working-classes is to belong to an all-pervading culture. . . ."[40]

2 Home-centeredness. The home and immediate family are the focus of life.[41]

3 Neighborhood-centeredness. Working class people live, shop, and often even work within a small area of the city, to which they are deeply attached. The neighborhood is a second home.[42]

4 "Them" versus "us" is a constant theme, the theme of the disadvantaged in-group against the cleverer or more powerful outsiders. The general attitude is that you can only trust your own sort.[43]

5 The personal and the concrete. Working class people attempt to humanize everything in their lives; they are rarely interested in theories or movements.[44]

6 The immediate, the present, the cheerful. Pleasure is given high priority; there is no real point in saving. These attitudes go along with a strong belief in luck or fate.[45]

The values or themes of the lower class subculture, as presented by Cohen and Hodges, are considerably different.

1 Simplification. Lower class people have experienced a relatively narrow range of objects and situations; their perspectives for defining and evaluating them are correspondingly narrow. Vicarious experience is not as easily available to them as it is to others.

2 Powerlessness in impersonal and achievement areas.

3 Deprivation. Lower class people feel more deprived than people on other levels, in this and many other studies.
4 Insecurity. The irregular and unpredictable occurrence of deprivation leads to feelings of insecurity. This is closely associated with pessimism.
5 Misanthropy. They feel that the world is a jungle.
6 Toughness. Much of lower class toughness is just talk, but this is in itself valued.
7 Anti-intellectualism and intolerance.[46]

Table 3 attempts to group and summarize the social class values or themes into common dimensions, using Williams' dominant (middle class) values as the starting point. When they are set forth in terms of this schema, it can be seen that there are meaningful relationships 1) between the social classes on a given value-dimension (reading horizontally), and 2) between the value-dimensions themselves for any given social class (reading vertically).

Note first that each value-dimension may logically be treated as a continuum (see Table 4) and that the three sets of social class values occupy successive positions along the continua. Each middle class value-dimension in Table 3 appears to represent a "plus" position relative to the comparable working class value-dimension: that is, the middle class values seem to be enlargements upon the working class themes. The latter may be considered to constitute a zero position or starting point for each continuum, while the lower class values seem to occupy a minus position—a defeated version, as it were, of working class values.

Note also that the values and themes for a given social class support one another and therefore can be considered to be a system. In fact a comparison of the two sets of value-dimensions, as presented in Table 4, suggests that the left-hand and right-hand items could be subsumed under rationalism and traditionalism respectively, or even under the broader summarizing concepts of

TABLE 3
The Patterning of Social Class Values or Themes

Middle Class Values	Value-Dimension	Working Class Values[1]	Lower Class Values	Value-Dimension
Active mastery Manipulation Open world-view; change, flux, movement	Activity	Striving for stability and security Belief in luck or fate	Powerlessness in impersonal and achievement areas	Passivity
Faith in rationalism Preference for orderliness	Rationalism	Traditionalism Attitudes held un-questioningly Pragmatism and anti-intellectualism Oral and local tradition	Anti-intellectualism and intolerance	Traditionalism
Universalistic ethic Stress on equality rather than hierarchy	Universalism	Person-centeredness Home and neighbor-hood centeredness The personal and the concrete	Simplification and narrow experience and perspectives	Particularism

Emphasis on individual personality	Individualism	Person-centeredness Home and neighborhood centeredness "Them" versus "us"	Deprivation Misanthropy	Primary group orientation
Strong orientation toward change and the future	Future Orientation	Excitement The immediate, the present, the cheerful No point in saving Belief in luck or fate	Toughness Insecurity	Present Orientation

[1] Both Miller and Reissman's and Hoggart's lists are included here.

TABLE 4
The Social Class Value-Dimensions
(Summary of Table 2)

Middle Class		Working Class/Lower Class
Activity	—	Passivity
Rationalism	—	Traditionalism
Universalism	—	Particularism
Individualism	—	Primary Group Orientation
Future Orientation	—	Present Orientation

Gesellschaft and *Gemeinschaft*. This suggests an interpretation of the origin of these social class differences which will be discussed in Chapter 6.

THE MAIN LINE TO PSYCHOLOGICAL MATURITY

To the extent that socialization of the individual into his social class subculture is successful, he will develop a number of personality attributes that embody that subculture.[47] It is possible to summarize these in terms of the degree of psychological maturity he has attained or his developmental level. In the same way the personality attributes characteristically found within a given social class can be examined for the degree of maturity that they represent, which may be termed the modal developmental level of that social class.

The concept of developmental level as used by social psychologists refers to all of the non-physical aspects of growth.[48] "The study of development . . . takes into consideration the progressive changes in each individual's adaptive functioning, with their consequent integration of constitutional and learned factors. Development in this sense refers to the multiple processes which are instrumental in forging each individual's personality."[49] Piaget has long held the position that the levels or stages of development are attained in an invariant sequential order, though the age at which a given stage is reached may vary in response to individual or cultural factors.[50] This position has never been seriously disputed. How the specific levels or stages are identified, described and labelled depends, of course, upon the particular interest of the investigator. His situation is much like that of the student of social class: where the boundary lines are drawn depends upon what factor is used as a measuring rod. Freud was interested in the affectional aspect of development, Erikson in identity formation, Piaget in the development of conceptual ability, and Witkin in perceptual ability, to name a few. Again as in the case of social class, there are strong correspondences between the various sets of stages worked out by these men. Erikson's first three ''phases,'' for example, correspond quite closely to Freud's oral, anal and genital stages.[51] But let's put these comparisons aside until Chapter 5 and concentrate here on the broader points of agreement about development and maturity.

One point of agreement has already been stated: that stages of development occur in a fixed sequential order, no matter how the stages are conceptualized. A second apparent convergence is that the various conceptualizations all seem to be aspects of a broad-scale underlying factor most usefully termed 'degree of stimulus-bondage.'[52] A number of other labels have been applied to it according to the investigator's focus of interest: motoric-conceptual,[53] field dependence-field independence,[54] concrete-abstract,[55] external control-internal control.[56] A reading of these studies shows that a motoric orientation is associated with field dependence, concreteness, and external control, and that all four may be assimilated to the concept of high stimulus-bondage. Similarly a conceptual orientation is linked with field independence, abstractness, internal control, and minimal stimulus-bondage. In other words these are interrelated aspects of the developmental process, just as occupation, income, and education are interrelated aspects of social class status.

The principal work out of which these concepts has grown is the study of child development. Given this empirical base it is not surprising that broad agreement should have been reached on the track the child must travel in order to reach maturity. Piaget's formulation of the process of cognitive development has gained wide acceptance and provides a model for other types of development as well. The young child in the "preoperational stage" reacts to and acts in terms of phenomenal reality only.[57] His actions are overt, sensorimotor ones. When he begins to make simple generalizations and to extend his thinking from the actual towards the potential, he has entered the stage of "concrete operations."[58] That is, he has interiorized and at the same time streamlined his actions, but they are still organized around concrete objects and events. These interiorized actions, now known as operations, must deal with factors one at a time for lack of an integrated system of higher-order generalizations. Also they continue to be more or less tied to perception. The stage of "formal operations" is normally reached in adolescence.[59] In this stage the mode of thinking is hypothetical-deductive. Concrete operations now serve as the basis for new classifications, new combinations of factors, and finally new propositions. Reality is seen in terms of its possibilities: its meaning for the future rather than just its meaning for the present. At this stage, then, the individual is no longer bound to the stimulus but is able to bend it to his own purpose.

Cognitive development is used as our model for personality development because it is the aspect which seems most relevant to social class. Its importance is signalled by the dominance of rationalism in the middle class value system—the dominant American value system. The preeminence of occupation as a criterion for social class placement and the correlation of educational with occupational status also underline the importance of cognitive development. Finally, while a high level of cognitive development can be achieved with only a low level of affective development, the reverse is not true, that a high level of affective development can be achieved with a low level of cognitive development. Erikson's highest stages of identity-formation, for example, involve such tasks as synthesizing the past and the future, taking on long-term responsibilities to others, and developing a philosophy of life[60]—none of which can be adequately accomplished by persons still in the stage of concrete operations. On the other hand, great intellectual achievements have been made by persons operating on a relatively low level of emotional maturity. Apparently cognitive development is basic to other aspects of personality growth. Since social class position involves social prestige, one would expect the most socially valued personality attributes to be found at the higher levels of the social class structure, just as the most highly valued occupational skills are. All other things being equal, therefore, a high level of cognitive development plus the emotional maturity which normally grows out of it should be found more frequently in high than in low social positions.

How is the mature personality described? The basic agreement upon the direction of personality development leads to general agreement upon the characteristics of maturity. In Werner's description cognitive and affective attributes are blended together as they are within personality.

[In the process of development] the organism becomes increasingly less dominated by the immediate concrete situation; the person is less stimulus-bound and less impelled by his own affective states. A consequence of this freedom is the clearer understanding of goals, the possibility of employing substitutive means and alternative ends. There is hence a greater capacity for delay and planned action. The person is better able to exercise choice and willfully rearrange a situation. In short, he can manipulate the environment rather than passively respond to [it]. . . . This freedom from the domination of the immediate situation also permits a more accurate assessment of others. The adult [for example] is more able than the child to distinguish between the motivational dynamics and the overt behavior of personalities. At developmentally higher levels, therefore, there is less of a tendency for the world to be interpreted solely in terms of one's own needs and an increasing appreciation of the needs of others and of group goals.[61]

PUTTING THEM TOGETHER

In Table 5 the five dimensions of the social class value systems presented in Tables 3 and 4 are lined up so as to correspond to Werner's list of the attributes of the mature personality.

The overall correspondence between Werner's attributes and the middle class value-dimensions is striking. Some question might arise as to the degree of correspondence in the last two categories. Yet universalism does involve a cognitive rather than an "appreciative" mode of orientation,[62] so it can reasonably be applied to an individual's understanding of psychological dynamics. Similarly, in the final comparison, when the reference to "others" and the "group" is extended beyond the primary group to include such entities as the community, the nation, and the world, individualism may be said to underlie them. Middle class individualism is not to be confused with self-centered, asocial hedonism. Rather it means "to be an autonomous and responsible agent, not merely a reflection of external pressures, and to have an internal center of gravity, a set of standards and a conviction of personal worth."[63] The conviction of personal worth carries with it the conviction of the personal worth of others, even those far removed from one's own in-groups, and therefore the psychological possibility of appreciating their needs.

Equally striking is the lack of correspondence between the attributes of maturity and the value-dimensions of the two lower classes. We saw earlier that the value-dimensions of the working

TABLE 5

A Comparison of Werner's Attributes of Maturity[1]
with Five Dimensions of Social Class Value Systems

Werner's Attributes of the Mature Personality	Dimensions of Middle Class Value System	Dimensions of Working and Lower Class Value System
Not dominated by immediate, concrete situation Capacity for delay and planning	Future Orientation	Present Orientation
Not driven by own affective states More intellectual approach to means and ends	Rationalism	Traditionalism
Active manipulation of the environment	Activity	Passivity
Accurate perception of others' motivations	Universalism	Particularism
Appreciation of needs of others and of group goals	Individualism	Primary Group Orientation

[1] Heinz Werner, "The Concept of Development from a Comparative and Organismic Point of View," in Dale B. Harris (ed.), *The Concept of Development* (Minneapolis: University of Minnesota Press, 1957), p. 127.

class represent a zero or beginning point on each scale, while those of the lower class seem to represent a minus position on several of the continua. Given the relationships set up in Table 5, the conclusion seems inescapable that from the social psychological point of view the social class hierarchy set forth here represents a developmental hierarchy as well. To put it another way, the modal developmental level within the three social classes is positively associated with their prestige ranking in American society.

According to this hypothesis, the social class value systems function to limit or facilitate the development of personality much as nutritional habits function to affect physical development. Children of all social classes start life in the same state of immaturity: insistent upon immediate gratification, blindly dependent upon familiar routines, unable to manipulate the environment themselves, and so on. However some will progress farther in the direction of maturity than others. The processes which make for developmental differentials at various levels of the social class structure constitute the subject matter of the next section of this book.

So far the developmental differences under consideration have been *modal* differences between social classes. What about the large number of cases on either end of the presumably normal curve? If the value-dimensions exist in the form of continua, and if the typical social class positions represent successive points on each continuum correlating with the social class hierarchy, then the *non-modal* value positions within any social class must logically overlap with those of the adjacent classes. A schematic illustration of this is shown in Figure 1.

The fact of extensive subcultural overlapping or continuity facilitates both upward and downward mobility. Stating it in terms of the hypothesis under consideration, the developmental processes through which individuals pass constitute a sorting device for the social class structure. A cogent illustration of the connection between subcultures and social class placement is provided in

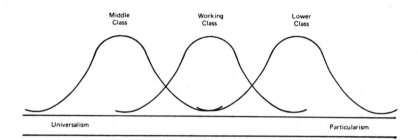

Figure 1. The Hypothetical Relationship of
Social Class Value Positions on Any One Dimension

Gans' *The Urban Villagers* when he describes two different life styles found in the same neighborhood.[64] The two types of people enacting them are referred to as "routine seekers" and "action seekers" and correspond generally to working class and lower class respectively.

The routine seekers desire above all a life of economic and emotional stability. Therefore their interaction patterns are characterized by rigid scheduling. There are regular menus for each day of the week, regular visiting routines, and regular holiday celebrations. The routine seekers are most likely to have stable skilled or semi-skilled jobs with adequate wages. They are thrifty, spending their extra money on the family or saving it for emergencies.

The action seekers, on the other hand, have jobs of minimal stability, skill and pay. This is partly cause and partly effect. "As their upbringing has not prepared them for work or interest in work, they often gravitate into the least satisfying jobs. This, in turn, encourages them even further to find gratification in episodes of action."[65] Their lives are episodic, spent for the most part in killing time except during the periodic adventurous episodes.

"The goal is action, an opportunity for thrills, and for a chance to face and overcome a challenge."[66] Impulsive spending is also characteristic of this group. The action seeker pattern is primarily a male one and is most apt to be found among adolescents and unmarried young men, although some continue the same pattern after marriage.

Gans' statement that in this neighborhood the action seekers represent a pattern of youth apparently means that many working class youths operate on the basis of lower class values for a time before adopting the values of their parents. From the point of view of mobility and social class selection, this means that those who as youths are characterized by an action-seeking or less mature set of values but who later adopt the stability-oriented values of their working class parents eventually become adult members of the working class. But those who continue on as action seekers become downwardly mobile and as adults become members of the lower class through their disinterest in acquiring work skills and their generalized need for immediate gratification. In this way the developmental level reached by an individual can direct him into the social class where he will find others most like himself in occupation, values and life style. This is an important mechanism through which subcultural differences between social classes are perpetuated.

CONCLUSION

Our first task has been to identify the major areas of agreement about social class. Occupation turned out to be the single most useful criterion, and four social classes seem to be indisputably recognized. These are the lower class, the working class, a conglomerate middle class, and a residual upper class. An adequate delineation of the upper class and general agreement on discriminations within the middle class sector await future work. Since the studies collated in this book seldom if ever deal with the upper class, it is not given further consideration.

Each of the three classes we are dealing with has a subculture which is epitomized in its value system. The values of any one class can be subsumed under five value-dimensions, each representing a continuum upon which each class occupies a different position. These value-dimensions or continua are: activity-passivity, rationalism-traditionalism, universalism-particularism, individualism-primary group orientation, and future orientation-present orientation. The relative positions of the three classes on the whole set of value-dimensions suggest that the middle class value system is an elaborated forward-looking version of the working class value system, while that of the lower class is a more constricted and negativistic version of it.

The major areas of agreement concerning the development of personality have also been described: the fixed order of developmental stages, the underlying factor or track along which development proceeds—degree of stimulus-bondage—and the definition of the mature, fully developed personality. A rather striking correspondence has been noted between certain levels of personality development and the relative positions of the three social classes along the five value-dimensions. On the basis of the patterning of this correspondence, it appears that the modal level of personality development in the three classes is positively correlated with their respective ranks in the social class hierarchy. To put it differently, the subculture of a given social class determines to a significant degree the developmental level of those socialized into it. Those socialized into subcultural values not congruent with their current social class position are candidates for mobility into a more appropriate social setting, in which they will be closer to the typical developmental level.

2

Learning How to Know

Social Class Differences

in

Cognitive Learning

To be convincing, the proposition that the typical level of personality development is directly related to social class position must be more than a logical construct. Empirical evidence is needed to support it, and this is abundant. More than 120 studies are reviewed in the next three chapters, somewhat arbitrarily collated under the headings of cognitive, affective and associational learning.* And just as significant as the sheer weight of the supporting evidence is the fact that no body of contradictory evidence has been found.

Cognitive learning involves learning how to acquire and use

---

*In the child's actual experience most learnings have both cognitive and affective components and involve social interaction. Cognitive learning is dealt with first because it is used here as the model for personality development (Chapter 1, pp. 22-23).

information, how to discriminate and generalize, how to think and communicate symbolically. It is hard to think of any class-related factors which could seriously constrain such a broadly based, pervasive developmental process, but several have been identified.

EARLY CHILDHOOD FACTORS

The importance of the mother in the child's emotional development has been so strongly emphasized in the past as to obscure her effect upon his cognitive development. Yet this begins even before he is born, according to investigations of the effect of prenatal nutrition upon measured intelligence. A study of identical twins found that the twin with the smaller birthweight was very likely to have a lower IQ than the other, presumably because of having received poorer nourishment.[1] Another study, involving 60,000 pregnant women and a follow-up of their children, found that the children of mothers who lost excessive amounts of protein through the kidneys during pregnancy had significantly lower IQ scores as preschoolers than the children of normal mothers.[2] The effect of prenatal malnutrition upon IQ seems to be due to its preventing the growth of the normal number of brain cells. Since no more brain cells are formed after the infant is six months old, malnutrition up to this age can permanently stunt the growth of the brain.[3] Recently, another factor has been implicated in the effect of prenatal and early postnatal malnutrition on learning ability. This is a deficiency in two chemical substances that carry impulses between neurons.[4] In other words malnutrition may lower the ability of the brain to function even when it does not actually stunt its growth.

Since malnutrition is generally due to poverty and ignorance, the lowering of cognitive ability by this factor is most likely to occur in the lower class and least likely in the middle class. Other physical factors which affect cognitive development are also beginning to be recognized. These include exposure to lead poisoning, air pollution, physical crowding, and noise. Once again it is lower class children who are most likely to experience them and therefore to suffer some deficit in cognitive development. Another approach to deficient cognitive development is to ask what physical effects culture may have upon the brain. Laboratory studies show that

> Permitting the young rat to grow up in an educationally and experientially inadequate and unstimulating environment creates an animal with a relatively deteriorated brain—a brain with a thin and light cortex, lowered blood supply, diminished enzymatic activities, smaller neuronal cell bodies and fewer glia cells. A lack of adequate educational fare for the young animal—*no matter how large the food supply or how good the family*—and a lack of psychological enrichment results in palpable, measurable deteriorative changes in the brain's chemistry and anatomy.[5] (Italics added)

While it is not possible to collect comparable anatomical information from children, behavioral evidence pointing in the same direction is abundant.

Some years ago a psychologist removed thirteen children from a state orphanage and placed each in the care of an adult ward at a neighboring institution for the retarded.[6] The children, all of them less than three years old, were clearly retarded; in fact, three were classified as imbeciles. The adult retardates were delighted with their new charges. "The wards competed," we are told, "to see which one would have its 'baby' walking and talking first." Meanwhile a control group of thirteen children remained at the orphanage and continued to be cared for by staff nurses in their usual speedy, efficient, rather depersonalized manner. Two years later the IQ's of the children cared for by the retarded adults had increased by 28 points on the average, while the control group at the orphanage, most of whom had been better off intellectually at the beginning of the experiment, had lost an average of 26 IQ points.

Now, thirty years later, four of the controls are in institutions of some kind, and those able to support themselves are in menial occupations. By contrast the entire experimental group is self-supporting, most of them in middle class occupations, and the 28 children born to them show no signs of retardation. The marked superiority of the experimental group in intelligence and general competence seems to be due to the personal attention and stimulation they received during a critical developmental period.

Another study of the effect of environmental stimulation involved the infants of forty lower class mothers with IQ's below 70.[7] Most of the families had no father in the home. Two-thirds of the children were given daily exposure to "a wide variety of mental stimulation on a one-to-one basis with a trained adult." The rest of the children, the control group, were left completely in the hands of their mothers. Three and a half years later the children exposed to stimulation had gained an average of 33 IQ points over the controls. The difference between normality and retardation, then, can be of environmental rather than of physical origin, though cultural deprivation ultimately has physical consequences within the brain. In any case mental retardation is most likely to be found at the bottom of the social class system, and this fact need not be attributed to "bad genes."[8]

Social class differences in maternal behavior and their consequences for children's competence have been strikingly described in a preliminary report of the Harvard School of Education's Pre-School Project.[9] First, a list of the abilities possessed by three-year-olds was developed on the basis of observation. Seventeen were identified, nine of which were intellectual and eight social. On the basis of these abilities the observed children were classified as "A" (highly competent), "B" (moderately competent), and "C" (incompetent). The A's and C's, a total of 440 children, were intensively studied for a year. Then a new group of

170 one to three-year-olds was selected for study, with the object of determining what experiences or lack of experiences could account for their differences in competence.[10] On the basis of extensive observation within the 170 homes, the Harvard group classified the mothers of A's and C's into five categories:

1 The *Super Mother*, who is constantly teaching the child and elaborating upon his experiences but who enjoys him at the same time. She is especially interested in developing the child's language. However, she does not push him unduly in any area and frequently follows his lead.

2 The *Smothering Mother*, who dominates the child and is never satisfied with his accomplishments.

3 The *Almost Mother*, who enjoys and accepts the child but who hasn't the capacity to lead the child beyond his current level. She tends to be unimaginative and easily confused.

4 The *Overwhelmed Mother*, who has very little time or energy for encouraging the child's development because she is too harassed by housekeeping or other problems.

5 The *Zoo Keeper Mother*, who is highly organized and efficient about physical caretaking but who has no time or interest in the child.

The Super-Mother turns out an A child. The Smothering Mother also turns out an A child so far as cognitive abilities are concerned, but her child is strikingly immature emotionally. The Almost Mother is most effective before the child is a year and a half old; after that his developmental curve flattens out and he becomes a B. The Overwhelmed Mother, and presumably the Zoo-Keeper as well, produce a C child.

While all types of mothers can be found in all social classes, the tendency is for middle class mothers to produce far more competent children than lower class mothers.[11] In the Harvard study the middle class child typically spent much more time than the lower class child in role-taking ("pretending"), practicing skills, and studying objects visually. At the other extreme the child of the Overwhelmed Mother, who was usually lower class, spent more of his time in eating, moving about aimlessly, or sitting and doing nothing.

Jerome Kagan reported after studying 180 white youngsters of the major social classes that "Class differences emerge clearly by 12 months of age, and show up even earlier for girls—in some cases as early as 8 months."[12] These differences were not confined to one or two key areas like language but appeared in all the basic skills the child was learning. Middle class children by the age of one year, for example, had better powers of discrimination than lower class children. They were also more attached to their mothers and so might be expected to be more receptive to their teachings.[13]

A study of mothers and their preschool children in an experimental situation[14] found no social class differences in the *desires* of mothers to have their children perform well. It was in their *behavior* that significant class differences appeared. As compared with blue-collar mothers, those of higher class did four times more directing, nine times more helping, five times more encouraging of independent thought and responsibility, and three times more teaching. Most impressive of all, the middle class mothers were observed to play with their children 250 times more than the mothers of lower class. This overall behavior pattern of the middle class mothers has been observed in other studies as well.[15] It strongly resembles that of the Super Mother and the Smothering Mother, both of whom produce cognitively superior children.

The Harvard group's conviction that differences in early child-rearing styles have long-range implications for intellectual development is supported by a study of sixty mothers of fifth grade children with similar IQ's.[16] When the children were divided into those with high verbal ability and those with low, it was found that the mothers of "highs" as compared with mothers of "lows" had given their children more verbal stimulation in early childhood, had bought more books for them, and had emphasized academic achievement. Observed in interaction with their children, the mothers of "highs" outdid the mothers of "lows" in all categories of helping behavior and of withholding help without showing disapproval, which may be considered a type of independence training. Presumably these techniques had been used ever since the children were very young. By the time they were ten or eleven, the children had developed high verbal ability, and a large part of this accomplishment must be credited to their talkative, stimulating, somewhat intrusive mothers.

Numerous studies made in the first half of this century affirmed the positive relationship between social class and verbal ability.[17] More recent studies expand the relationship to include conceptual ability as well. Middle class children perform better not only on verbal tasks[18] but also on non-verbal sorting problems requiring some ability to think abstractly.[19] In general they show a strong preference for concepts over concrete material as compared with children of lower class.[20] One interesting sidelight is that there appears to be more variation in the conceptual ability of blue-collar than of white-collar children; while the latter's scores cluster at the high end of the scale, those of the former show considerable scatter.[21] Whether the high-scoring blue-collar children have had an upbringing more similar to that of the average middle class child or whether they have developed their ability in spite of a typical blue-collar upbringing is not known. The results of similar studies of black children are consonant with those just described,[22] social class once again outweighing race.

If a helpful, encouraging, mutually enjoyable relationship between mother and child produces superior cognitive development, then a threatening, authoritarian relationship should have the opposite effect. Studies show that the latter type is more likely to be found in blue-collar than in white-collar families. Its subcultural foreshadowing can be found in the tendency of blue-collar women to define pregnancy as a form of sickness.[23] The favoring of retaliatory child-rearing methods is very significantly related to this attitude,[24] and so it is not surprising that the later use of command, threat, and other coercive techniques turn out to be more typical of blue-collar than of white-collar parents.[25] There is evidence that parental power-assertion of this kind may not only disrupt the child's cognitive learning but may also push the child toward resisting or rejecting the parents' teachings for emotional reasons.[26] To the extent that the parent-child relationship is coercive or threatening, then, the child will be harder to train at home and probably at school.

The same pattern of social class differences in power-assertion is found in the relationships of black mothers and children. In a study of black mothers of four-year-olds, half of whom were lower class and the other half middle class, the latter were found more likely to initiate interaction with the child and to show affection, verbally and non-verbally.[27] Further, only 12 percent of their techniques could be classified as commanding-without-explanation, while 35 percent of the techniques of lower class black mothers fell into this category and an additional 6 percent were classified as threats or warnings. As Hess puts it in summarizing his study of similar groups,

> . . . . teaching styles of [black] mothers in the working class*
> [as compared with those of middle class black mothers] seem
> to be socializing a passive attitude toward learning on the part
> of the child in which his own imagination, curiosity, and
> assertiveness are discouraged, and he is taught to assume the
> stance of waiting to be told, to receive, and to be acted
> upon.[28]

*This probably includes lower class mothers too, but the reference is not clear.

Here is additional evidence that the effects of the social class subcultures supersede those of the racial subcultures and thus that cognitively underdeveloped children of both racial groups are most likely to come from lower class homes.

LINGUISTIC STYLE AND
CONCEPTUAL DEVELOPMENT

Language can give the child the means of escaping from stimulus-bondage by providing him with the tools for mentally modelling and remodelling his world. On the other hand it can bind him tightly to his culture by presenting the world in narrowly ethnocentric terms. Both of these conditions, independence and bondage, are rooted in stubborn physiological fact. If the child is ever to become independent of stimuli, he must begin by acquiring the basic verbal abilities in the nursery years, when the neurons in the brain are making their most rapid spurt of growth and establishing connections with other cells. Once he reaches kindergarten age, the rate of growth within the brain slows down, and the commitment to a particular way of thinking becomes neurally established.[29] "Thereafter [it] will exercise a controlling influence on all future perceptions, judgments, motives and behaviors."[30] If his way of thinking is a conceptual one, encouraging the manipulation of ideas, the child can gradually become the master of his environment. If it is a concrete, motorically dominated style, he is likely to remain in bondage to his cultural and physical world. Language or linguistic style is a basic determinant of cognitive development.

The British sociologist Bernstein studied social class linguistic differences among school children in an attempt to explain how they affect children's personality development and school performance.[31] He found that the children of semi-skilled and unskilled workers characteristically use an impressionistic, noninstrumental approach to social relations and social objects, whereas middle class children (a category so defined that it would include some American working class families) use a more systematic and structural approach. Lower class children are sensitive to content because they have learned to respond to the boundaries of an object. Middle class children are sensitive to structure because they have learned to respond to the matrix of relationships in which an object is embedded. The determinant of each of these cognitive styles, Bernstein believes, is a particular linguistic style: a "public language" in the case of lower class children and a "formal language" in the case of middle class children. He sees these two linguistic styles not as dichotomies, but as stages on a continuum, public language being at the lower developmental end.[32]

A public language uses short, grammatically simple, often unfinished sentences, many short commands and questions, rigid and limited use of adjectives and adverbs. It seldom uses an impersonal pronoun as the subject of a conditional sentence, and its symbolism is of a low order of generality. Personal qualification is left out of the structure of the sentence, making the public language one of implicit rather than explicit meaning. Since feelings can be only crudely described, they have to be communicated by changes in volume and tone, gesture, and expression. Thus the lower class child comes to rely heavily upon the non-verbal aspects of communication: the concrete and motoric. The frequent resort to hackneyed epithets and euphemisms is probably the result of the lack of a more exact vocabulary and syntax of affect. These clichés obscure the speaker's meaning even from himself, but they have the advantage of requiring little or no thought on the part of either speaker or listener. It is significant, Bernstein feels, that public language has more terms of this kind than formal language has.[33] Similarly, the frequent use of set traditional phrases like "It's only natural, isn't it?" sets up a sympathetic circularity in the social relationship and discourages an analytical consideration of the subject matter. Such global, undiscriminating responses to the environment are characteristic of a public language. Those qualifications that are made are social or consensual rather than individual, producing a press toward uniformity of expression and behavior within the lower class group.[34]

This linguistic style has consequences for the lower class child's conceptual development as well as for his social relationships. There is some evidence that the percentage of nouns to verbs is higher in the public than in the formal language, suggesting that things get more attention than processes.[35] Poor use of verbs is one of the specific characteristics noted in American culturally deprived children.[36] The public language is often insensitive to the appropriate tense of the verb, indicating disregard for or confusion in time orientation.[37] The time perspective is short and tends to stress the present over the future.[38] Reliance on a small group of conjunctions, mainly "and," "so," "then," and "because," and on simple sentence construction inhibits the logical development of thought.[39] Only the crudest causal connections are made. This factor, along with the short time perspective, tends to fragment the lower class child's experience and lead him away from the perception of structural relationships.[40] His failure to use impersonal pronouns is both the cause and the effect to his confinement within his own personal experiences and local situations;[41] he is bound by immediate, concrete stimuli.

The middle class child learns a public language from his peers and a formal language from his parents and teachers. The formal language is characterized by accurate grammar and syntax, logical modifications and emphasis mediated through the use of subordinate clauses, frequent use of impersonal pronouns, discriminating selection from a wide range of adjectives and adverbs, and explicit verbal qualification of individual meaning.[42] The fact that this linguistic style encourages the individualization of both affective and cognitive expression suggests a more individualized and more creative personality in those who use it. The fact that it encourages abstraction and generalization suggests a more rational approach to experience. The picture of the typical middle class personality which begins to emerge is that of a well developed one.

None of the evidence of American studies contradicts in any way Bernstein's observations and formulations. Walter Miller has described the "non-school grammatical system" of American lower class teenagers as similar to the public language of British lower class children.[43] Riessman's study of culturally deprived American children[44] describes their cognitive style in terms which effectively summarize Bernstein's inferences:

1 physical and visual rather than aural,
2 spatial rather than temporal,
3 content-centered rather than form-centered,
4 externally oriented rather than introspective,
5 problem-centered rather than abstract-centered,
6 inductive rather than deductive,
7 slow, careful, patient, and persevering in areas of importance, rather than quick, clever, and facile,
8 expressively rather than instrumentally oriented.

An American study of adults not only corroborates Bernstein's work but goes beyond it.[45] This analysis of taped interviews with the survivors of an Arkansas tornado showed that the linguistic style of lower class respondents severely limited their ability to comprehend their own situation, let alone that of others.

For one thing, the perspective of the lower class respondent was extremely narrow. Almost without exception he described through his own eyes, even when supposedly reconstructing events and portraying the feelings of others. He could not seem to put himself in another person's shoes. Interaction was not taken account of and was barely implied: e.g., "We run over there to see about them, and they was alright." This is a manifestation of what Piaget calls egocentrism, by which he means being embedded in one's own point of view, an indicator of cognitive immaturity.[46] By contrast the middle class respondent was able to describe an event from any of several standpoints: that of another person, a class of persons, an organization, an organizational role, or a town. Even descriptions of his own behavior were sometimes portrayed from other points of view.[47]

Taking the role of the listener was as hard for the lower class respondent as taking the role of another survivor of the disaster. He could not "hear" his words as others heard them and egocentrically assumed that his imagery corresponded with that of his listener. He seldom qualified his statements and frequently used unclear referents like "we" and "they." His remarks therefore tended to be quite general without ever becoming generalizations or summary statements. The middle class respondent, on the other hand, rarely failed to locate his image in space and time. He used multiple perspectives and showed great sensitivity to his listeners, both actual and potential. He used many devices to supply context and clarify meaning: rich introductory material, frequent illustrations, anticipation of disbelief, and complex identifying detail. In short the middle class subject was less stimulus-bound, in that he was able to stand outside of his experience and regard it objectively.[48]

The lower class respondent seemed unsure of classifications and resorted to dichotomies such as rich and poor, hurt and unhurt. Classificatory terms were rudimentary and relationships between them left vague. Questions about organizations such as the Red Cross were converted into concrete terms like "the helping people," and there seemed to be little or no understanding of where particular organizations fit into the social structure of the community. All of this is probably related to the lack of qualifying statements mentioned earlier and represents the global rather than differentiated response which Bernstein says is a characteristic of a public language.[49] The middle class respondent handled classifications with ease, often explicitly relating one category to another.

The use of concrete imagery was overshadowed by the prevalence and richness of conceptual terminology.[50]

Lower class stylistic devices were more segmental or limited in scope than middle class ones. Personal narratives were the preferred form, and much wandering from the main track was noted. The relating of one incident triggered the recollection of another. Thus there was no systematic elaboration but only a shotgun listing of images and incidents. Middle class respondents, however, imposed overall frameworks of their own on the interview, and within these master settings they introduced subsidiary ones. They were able to elaborate on a theme without losing it and made rich parallel comparisons followed by a return to the original point. In short their complex yet flexible stylistic devices enabled them to gain a better understanding of their own experience and that of others.[51]

The lower class child, then, is reared by parents and relatives whose linguistic style and conceptual limitations confine them for the most part within their own personal experiences and within immediate, local situations. The social class differences in child-rearing will be described at length in the next chapter, since child-rearing is so largely concerned with affective (moral) interpretations of the child's cognition and behavior. Suffice to note here that the power-assertive style, whose consequences for the child's cognitive development were pointed out earlier, seems to be based upon this preoccupation with the personal and the immediate. The authority for a statement or directive is seen as deriving from the status differential within the social relationship rather than from reasoned principles. When the child is told he cannot go out, for example, and asks why, he is likely to be answered, ''Because I said you can't; now shut up!'' Bernstein has pointed out that any challenge to a statement of this kind represents an attack upon legitimate authority and thus it justifies a moralistic retaliation. The child who is frequently managed by this method will come to have rebellious and highly emotionalized attitudes toward authority generally.[52] Other ascribed statuses that tend to be used in managing the lower class child are age, sex, religion, and ethnicity. For example, "You aren't old enough to have a jack-knife"; "Boys don't play with dolls"; "Don't act like a lousy (whatever)". Middle class parents, because they place high importance upon the child's individuality, are more likely to modify the status demands of their subculture by taking his feelings and preferences into account.[53] They are also more likely to give rational explanations for their statements since they have better information, the means to convey it, and the motivation to do so. The child-rearing style of any social class represents one application of its linguistic and cognitive style to a problem area, and so it is predictably congruent with them.

Language is the distinctively human ingredient of thought, interaction, and personality. If this ingredient is rich in variety and complex in structure, its users can convert it into products that reflect these qualities. If it is of limited variety and simple structure, its users have fewer kinds of materials with which to build. Therefore linguistic style sets the developmental limits for cognitive style.

MOTORIC EXPRESSION: AN ALTERNATIVE TO CONCEPTUAL EXPRESSION

To the child nothing is more personal, concrete, and immediate than his own body, and he delights in using it. Because motoric expressiveness is strongest in infancy and dwindles somewhat in importance as the child learns to use language to get what he wants, a motoric orientation or preference is said to represent a lower developmental level than a verbal orientation. Which mode becomes dominant in the personality of the child depends to a considerable extent upon the subculture in which he grows up. If the subculture emphasizes and rewards the 'conversation of gestures' over the communication of thought, the child will prefer motoric expression. If in addition the linguistic style of his subculture is rigid and narrow, the earlier mode of expression will not be superseded in later years.

Social class differences in motoric development have been noted in infancy, with working and lower class black babies showing significant acceleration over middle class black babies.[54] This is associated with their mothers' not subjecting them to physical restraint nor pushing them to transform motor activities into motor skills. Among white mothers the less educated give their infants significantly more physical stimulation than verbal and/or visual stimulation, which are preferred by the better educated mothers.[55]

The same pattern of social class differences was found in a study which asked the parents of junior high school children how they liked the youngsters to spend their leisure time.[56] Middle class parents clearly preferred that their children engage in activities of a conceptual nature, while working and lower class parents preferred motoric activities for theirs. Although the children themselves showed no significant social class difference in preferring one over the other type of leisure time activity, when it came to future occupations the middle class children chose conceptually oriented ones significantly more often than the working and lower class children did. The same group of children was tested for ability to express emotion in two experimental settings. Predictably the middle class children performed much better in a conceptual than in a motoric situation, while the reverse was true of the blue-collar children.

A subsequent study by other investigators showed equally significant social class differences of the same type.[57] On five comparisons involving hobby preferences, job expectations, and so on, the working class boys expressed more motoric preferences than the middle class boys. Three of the five comparisons were significant below the .05 level.[58] When the boys were asked t⌷

play a modified game of "Statues" in which they were to portray emotional states such as fear, working class boys were found to be more motorically expressive, moving much more freely than the middle class boys.[59] The more conceptual approach of the middle class boys was evident in their superior performances on tasks such as abstract painting and fitting blocks into a frame.[60] Taken together, these studies support Bernstein's position that the conversation of gestures plays a much more important part in lower class communication than in that of the middle class.[61]

So far as child-rearing styles were concerned, mothers who used psychological discipline and symbolic rewards and who controlled their emotion during discipline produced the most conceptually oriented sons. Mothers who used corporal punishment had the most motorically oriented sons.[62] We shall see in the next chapter that these two different child-rearing styles tend to be found in the white-collar and blue-collar groups respectively.

Another way of approaching the question of motoric versus conceptual or verbal expression is by using the concept of field dependence and independence. This is the degree of ability to separate an object perceptually from its context or background and so to overcome the influence of one's surroundings. Witkin and his associates have developed a number of tests of this factor.[63] In the Rod-and-Frame Test the individual is placed in a dark room and shown a luminous frame tilted at an angle. His task is to move a luminous rod within it into a vertical position. A large deviation from true verticality indicates dependence upon the field, while a small deviation indicates relative independence. Other tests use such devices as a tilting chair and a tilting room.

In some of Witkin's early experiments 270 children of various ages served as subjects.[64] A major finding was that between the ages of ten and thirteen there is a sharp increase in field independence, and so this end of the continuum is considered to represent the higher maturity level.[65] This is apparently because field inde-

pendence involves analytical thought,[66] and early adolescence is
the age when many children acquire this ability, according to
Piaget and Erikson.[67]

For the purposes of this chapter the most interesting aspect of
Witkin's work is his correlation of field dependence and independence with adult personality characteristics. In a recent summary
of his work he describes field dependent adults as follows:

> These people are likely to change their stated views on a
> particular social issue in the direction of the attitudes of an
> authority. . . . Their impressions of people are usually based
> on the physical characteristics these people show and the
> actions they engage in. . . . When shown a TAT picture that
> portrays an aggressive act, field-dependent people are likely
> to give immediate expression to the ideas and feelings of
> aggression stimulated by the picture. . . . [68]

> [They] have a less developed sense of their identity and of
> their separateness from others than do most field-independent
> perceivers. . . . [69]

> The characteristics cited . . . reflect the quality of the person's
> experience of his surroundings, his way of perceiving and
> using his body, the nature of his relation to other people, and
> aspects of his controls and defenses. . . . [They] suggest
> consistency in psychological functioning which pervades the
> individual's perceptual, intellectual, emotional, motiva-
> tional, defensive, and social operation.[70]

Witkin did not use social class as a variable in his studies, and so
any connection between field dependence and low social status
must remain on a purely inferential level. Keeping this reservation
in mind, it is interesting to note that most of the characteristics of

field-dependent people could be predicted from the blue-collar value-dimensions presented in Chapter 1. Changing one's views to agree with those of an authority sounds like traditionalism. Judging other people on the basis of their physical characteristics is being dominated by concrete experience and being relatively passive and unanalytical in processing one's visual perceptions. Expressing motorically the feelings elicited by a picture sounds like impulsivity or a present orientation. Having less sense of separateness from others is having a (primary) group orientation rather than an individualistic one. These similarities strongly suggest that working and lower class people are more field dependent than middle class people.

At once, however, this suggestion is seen to produce a paradox. If blue-collar people prefer motoric to conceptual expression, as previously described studies seem to show, how can they also be field-dependent? Since motorically oriented people are presumably more competent in the use of the body than conceptually oriented people, surely they should be better able to resist the influence of a tilted perspective. Fortunately there is a study which seems to provide an answer to this problem.

When professional dancers were given Witkin's three perceptual tests, their performances were not significantly better than those of the original college student subjects, although they were slightly more inclined to be field-independent.[71] No relationship appeared between amount of dancing experience and performance in the perceptual tests, but the same correlations were found between personality scores and perceptual scores. Thus a natural aptitude for muscular control and balance plus years of practice had only a small effect on perceptual style. This conclusion supports in a particularly convincing way Witkin's claim that he is delineating the relationship of broad features of the personality to a characteristic way of perceiving.[72] It also answers the objection that motorically oriented people should ''naturally'' be more field-independent, since it shows that the association between a person's perceptual and his expressive style does not depend upon the state of his muscular coordination or motoric skills.

In a second study bearing upon this question, the literature on motoric inhibition and ideational functioning was reviewed, and two intriguing ideas emerged.[73] First, it appeared that inhibition of action could not occur before a certain level of development was reached, and therefore that motoric expression represents a lower developmental level than conceptual or ideational expression. Further, there was reason to believe that as the direct motoric gratification of impulses is increasingly inhibited, activity is correspondingly displaced from the motoric to the ideational sphere.

To test these notions directly two groups of subjects were selected. The motoric group was composed of chronically assaultive criminals; the verbal group consisted of psychiatric patients with a history of threatening to assault but of never carrying out these threats in action. Both groups were "pure" in the sense that they had no other conditions which might affect their responses, such as perversions, mania, or depression. They were given Rorschachs and the results were analyzed in terms of developmental level, using an index of integrative perceptual activity, and in terms of displacement to the ideational sphere, using the M score. The verbal group scored significantly higher than the motoric group on both counts. Also the motoric group gave significantly more responses characteristic of developmentally early thought processes. An analysis of case history material showed the verbal group to have more social attainments than the motoric group. Thus all of the evidence pointed to the lower developmental level of the motoric group, and this condition-was not restricted to their assaultive behavior but showed up in all areas of activity. The investigator concluded that it represented a generalized social inadequacy.[74]

Two related studies have been made of normal children. In a test of motor-impulse control, preschoolers from lower class families were asked to draw on paper a straight line between two X's and also to walk along a straight line.[75] Under the experimental condition "as slowly as possible," it was found that the child's ability to control his response correlated with his IQ. In the words of the investigators, "Motor control per se contributes to variation in Stanford-Binet performance."[76] The child who always reacts quickly may not be able to slow down enough to process the necessary information in an efficient way. Apparently, then, effective problem-solving requires not only conceptual ability but also the ability to withhold immediate response. The relation of this ability to social class is shown in a study which found blue-collar boys responding significantly faster on all but one verbal task than white-collar boys.[77] The blue-collar boys were eager to start and too busy to listen to instructions; thus they sacrificed accuracy to immediacy. By not taking time to think, they also produced less elaborated and less well organized responses. It is easy to see how this impulsive habit of response can impede the growth of intelligence and personality.

These studies suggest a further explanation for the professional dancers' tendency to be field-independent rather than field-dependent. Certainly a major difference between dancers and motorically oriented people is their ability to inhibit their motor impulses. The dancers have learned to control and purposefully direct their motoric activity——in fact to conceptualize it——while the ordinary motoric performer reacts unthinkingly with the means of expression most immediately available to him. The factors of internal control and conceptual manipulation make the crucial difference. These factors translate into rationalism and (conceptualized) activity, value-dimensions found at the upper end of the developmental scale.

ROLE-TAKING ABILITY

The child's ability to take the roles of others is based upon his understanding and use of language.[78] What begins as simple imitation of a model's physical gestures evolves into a cognitive and affective understanding of their meaning. When the child is able to imitate the model's verbal gestures as well, he is able to grasp the other's role as a Gestalt. There are three developmental consequences of this new understanding. First, he can become the other by mentally taking his role, a significant advance over the imitation of concrete acts. Second, in taking the role of the other toward himself, he becomes conscious of himself as a separate person. Third, he acquires a primitive understanding of motivations and relationships as he watches the model play different roles with different people, and so he can begin to imagine how the other would act in various situations. The behavior of others is now more understandable.

While the child is in the egocentric stage of believing that his perceptions are objectively accurate, he is field-dependent, passively subject to his perceptions rather than actively manipulating them. When confronted with a Piagetian problem such as this: "There are some cows, some sheep, and some chickens in a field. Are there more cows than chickens?", he is likely to answer "More cows," on the basis of their larger size.[79] His egocentrism also limits his ability to take the role of the other. He cannot readily shift from one way of looking at a situation to another until he has some conceptual schema with which to do so. In the case of the animal problem, this is an abstract counting system which enables him to ignore size. In the case of role-taking, it may be a set of role structures composed of generalizations about "mother," "mailman," or "dog" which enable him to construct their counterparts within himself. With these he can predict how these actors will feel in a situation and therefore how they will behave.

The cognitive and developmental aspects of role-taking have been experimentally demonstrated in studies of both children and adults. The "Role-Taking Test"[80] used in the three following studies makes use of a series of varied background scenes and a set of figures of men, women, and children. The subject is asked to tell a story for each of the three backgrounds using at least three figures in each story. Later he is asked to tell the stories again, this time from the point of view of each figure. The test is scored on two counts: the level of abstraction used to describe the actors and the degree of success in presenting the actors' perspectives. In the first study of sixty-eight boys who were given the Role-Taking Test and four of Piaget's cognitive tasks, the older boys performed better on both than the younger ones.[81] The experimenter also noted a concordance between subjects' performances on both types of task. These findings substantiate the idea that role-taking ability is related to cognitive ability and that both abilities are aspects of developmental level. More conclusive evidence is provided by a study of adults[82] which divided them into two groups on the basis of their Rorschach scores: those on a relatively high level of cognitive development and those on a relatively low level. A significant difference between the two groups was found in their Role-Taking Test scores, while no relationship appeared between these scores and age, education, or vocabulary score.

A third study administered the Role-Taking Test to 136 boys between the ages of ten and twenty one.[83] They had been selected out of a much larger group previously tested for their level of conceptual functioning according to Harvey, Hunt and Schroder's procedure, so that the experimental group consisted of four subgroups, each representing a different level of functioning. The finding which is of interest here is that at all levels of age and intelligence the boys with higher conceptual development were more skillful in taking the roles of others than those at lower developmental levels.

A study of 300 children in grades 2 through 8 tested the relation of conceptual ability to role-taking ability by means of the Abstract-Concrete Word Association Test.[84] This contains 48 items, each consisting of a noun as stimulus word and a noun plus a noun or adjective or verb as response choices. Role-taking ability was tested by asking three separate groups of children at each grade level to respond to the stimulus word with the words they thought other children would use. In one group children were asked to choose a response they thought first or second graders would choose to go with the stimulus word. In another group they were asked to choose a response that adults would prefer. In a third group in each grade they were to choose their own responses. Second and third graders were found to be practically unable to discriminate between these three age roles. From the fourth grade up, however, fewer abstract responses were chosen for the younger child role and more for the adult role than for the respondents themselves. These differences became significant at the fourth grade level and grew in magnitude at higher grade levels, a clear indication of the association between role-taking ability and developmental level. An interesting sidelight of this study is the finding that children's ability to distinguish and reproduce the adults' more abstract style does not coincide with their adoption of it.

Social class was not one of the variables investigated in the studies reported in this section. It is reasonable to expect, however, from the link between role-taking ability and conceptual ability that both of these would be at a higher level in the middle class than in the two lower classes. And in fact the lower class survivors of an Arkansas tornado reportedly had difficulty in taking the role of the listener and that of another survivor.[85] This can be explained on the basis of a restricted linguistic style, egocentrism, or a concretistic type of cognitive functioning, all of which are closely related. It can be attributed to social structural factors such as the diffuse, holistic nature of lower class role relationships.[86] A related explanation would involve the primary group orientation of working and lower class people and the relatively small size of their role repertory, which restricts their role-playing and role-taking experience. Gans puts it this way:

The person-oriented self, found in a social system in which social intercourse is restricted to familiar people, has less need to be empathic. . . . The origins of the person-oriented self [are related] to child-rearing practices. . . . Since there is little deliberate teaching by [blue-collar] parents, and since the child therefore learns mostly by imitation, he has few opportunities to learn self-consciousness, or to develop a self-image. . . . [He is] not likely to see people take someone else's point of view.[87]

Each type of explanation contributes something toward an understanding of the processes by which social class differences in role-taking ability may be produced and maintained.

CONCLUSION

The mother's influence on the child's cognitive development starts in the prenatal period with the adequacy of the nourishment she provides for him. Malnutrition at this stage or during the first six months of infancy can impair the functioning of the brain or even permanently stunt its growth. Certain cultural factors such as insufficient stimulation seem to have similar effects, to the point where they may produce mental retardation. Since the cultural factors and malnutrition are most likely to be found in the lower class and least likely in the middle class, the chances of suffering some degree of mental deficit increase as social class status decreases.

Even if the basic conditions for optimum cognitive development were met in all cases, social class differences would still occur because of differences in linguistic style. This factor is crucial whether viewed from the aspect of personality development or from that of the social class value systems. In terms of stimulus-bondage, the linguistic style which Bernstein calls public language has been shown to be so limited in vocabulary and syntax that it offers little help in abstract thinking. Thus, those who use it tend to remain on the concrete level of operation, dependent upon the perceptual field and dominated by the immediate stimulus. Because the public language is full of generalities and clichés, its users come to rely upon non-verbal cues like tone of voice and motoric behavior in order to convey or to grasp the meaning of a message. In fact they learn to prefer motoric expression in many areas of activity. Since the body is at once a concrete stimulus and an agent of concrete response, a motoric orientation represents a high degree of stimulus-bondage. Therefore exposing a child exclusively to public language would severely limit his personality development by keeping him at the concrete, stimulus-bound end of the developmental continuum. We have seen that the public language is used most commonly in the two lower classes.

The middle class child's experience is quite different. Although he learns the public language at an early age, he also learns the expanded and elaborated form called formal language, and this becomes the more important mode of communication. Possessed of a rich vocabulary and syntax, he can manipulate the environment both mentally and existentially. To the extent that he can operate in abstract terms, he can free himself from the immediate stimulus, whether it is located in the field or within his own body. His use of formal language is so rewarding that he comes to prefer verbal to motoric expression except where the latter is perceived as symbolic of his conceptualizations. In this way the linguistic style preferred by the middle class individual enables him to move toward developing his full potential in personality.

Turning from personality to subculture, a similarly supportive relationship between the characteristic linguistic style of a social class and its value-system is apparent. The linguistic factors that produce a high degree of stimulus-bondage in the blue-collar individual are reflected in such cautious value-dimensions as passivity and primary group orientation. The middle class individual escapes this by using his more flexible linguistic style to dominate his environment, and so he comes to value activity. Recognizing the usefulness of abstract thought, he also espouses rationalism, while the working class individual adopts a less self-confident traditionalism. These rival values carry with them a commitment to change (orientation toward the future) on the one hand, and to a conservative stability (orientation toward the present) on the other. They are maintained by the full, accurate use of verb tenses and long time perspective in the formal language of the middle class and by the elision of verb tenses and time sequences in the public language of the blue-collar groups.

Role-taking ability is strongly affected by two additional value-dimensions. People who are steeped in the highly subjective primary group values of affective interaction and conformity to group norms cannot be expected to perceive the needs and motivations of others as well as people who can take a more rational, objective view—even of their own subjective experiences. Middle class people learn a language which makes frequent use of impersonal pronouns, the conditional tense, and generalizations. Thus it supports universalism, a value which sensitizes its holders to the kind of similarities between people that lead to accurate generalizations about their needs and motivations. In doing so it leads the typical middle class person away from the naively egocentric perspective which handicaps many working and lower class people in taking the roles of others.

The fifth value-dimension, individualism, is in a sense the personal reward awaiting those who live up to the rest of the middle class creed: the freedom to develop one's personality in whatever subculturally approved areas one wishes and the applause of others for doing so. It has been noted that the individualization of meaning is possible in the formal language but impossible in the public one. The individualization of expression and of personality also depend upon access to a broader range of experience than is available in primary groups. The broader the range of experience, both personal and vicarious, the stronger the tendency to have universalistic perceptions of others and the greater the ability to take their roles. The greater the ability to take the roles of others, the more models are available for developing various facets of the personality, thus increasing the ability to become psychologically independent. Empathy and autonomy come together in individualism. All of this supports the proposition that developmental level and social class position are systematically related.

3

Learning How
to Behave

Social Class Differences

in

Affective Learning

While learning about the world involves the development of cognitive skills, learning how to behave in it is primarily an affective experience. In terms of content it consists of learning the norms and values of the social class subculture. In terms of personality it consists of learning how to be good and bad, socially acceptable and rejectable—in the broadest sense, moral development.

How the child is taught may be even more important than what he is taught. The same content can be presented concretely or abstractly, repressively or in an evocative manner. Since the parents have the greatest access to the child during the critical years, their cognitive and affective styles become determining factors in the child's development.

Furthermore, the child's training is virtually complete before he has developed the cognitive skills to look at it objectively. The very young child can only learn the subculture on the basis of imitation and conditioning. Even when he becomes able to grasp the rules of conduct, he understands them in a concrete way as sacred laws existing outside of human beings and operating inexorably like the law of gravity. Only after the age of ten or eleven, when he begins to think conceptually, does the middle class child become capable of regarding the subcultural norms and values as manmade guidelines subject to criticism and change.[1] And since the level of cognitive development correlates with social class level, many children of lower status will not be able to do so until even later, if ever.

IMITATION AND IDENTIFICATION

The earliest form of cultural or subcultural learning is imitation. Its effectiveness is limited by the fact that the young child is not able to copy any and all the behaviors of another person but only those he has already approximated in practice. Imitation is not mere copying of another's behavior but is the active reshaping of one's own behavior.[2] When the imitative behavior is rewarded, it tends to be repeated and perfected. This shaping of imitation is the first step in the child's acculturation.

A still stronger foundation for the internalization of norms and values is laid down when the child begins to identify with his parents. Modern explanations of identification base the process upon three elements, the first of which is the child's ability to be conscious of himself as separate from, though related to others.[3] This is made possible by the learning of language, which enables the child to think about the relationships between various persons and aspects of persons by using words like "I," "me," "he," "him," "they," and "them."[4] The rudiments of role-playing are apparent here. Second, the child must perceive the person he is identifying with as possessing a somewhat generalized competence that he himself would like to possess. Thus identification is a special form of imitation which goes beyond wanting to *do* something just like someone else and means wanting to *be* like that someone else.[5] Third, the child must feel ambivalent toward his model, experiencing "various combinations of love, tenderness, fear, and hate."[6] These feelings, which grow out of his perception of the model's competence and power, force the child to anticipate whether a contemplated action will please or displease him. In other words, the child learns to carry on an internalized interaction with the model, to consider his own behavior in advance, and thus eventually to control it.

Evidently the parent-child relationship most likely to facilitate identification with the parents is one which provides a good deal of verbal interaction, helping and teaching by the parent, and the acceptance of negative as well as positive feelings. It's the type of relationship described in the last chapter as facilitating the development of verbal and conceptual ability and as being more frequently found in middle class families than in those of lower status.

The first identification formed by children is usually with the mother. The fact that girls are not expected later to shift this primary identification to another model undoubtedly helps to account for the fact that their development is generally easier than that of boys. As they are growing up, girls show more social skill, are more stable emotionally, and generally seem more mature at a given age than boys. They are more successfully acculturated, tending to be more conventional and less deviant at all ages. Boys, by contrast, are required to break away from identification with the mother at a rather early age in order to establish their maleness. They must give up their psychic unison with her and learn counterpoint. The quickest and most effective way of accomplishing this is by identification with the father, evidence of which usually begins to appear by the age of three[7] if it is to appear at all.

Learning to take on the father's characteristics and give up those of the mother presents different problems at each social class level.

Middle class boys need not make a complete break with the mother, because sex roles in the middle class are less sharply differentiated. Indeed there is increasing continuity between them. On the other hand the middle class boy finds his father's occupational activities harder to understand than the boy of lower social class, because they are based upon the manipulation of people and concepts rather than of things. While his sister is readily learning the female role by watching and helping her mother, the middle class boy is struggling to model himself upon a man whose most important activities are obscure. If he has little support in this (for example, constant urging to be himself rather than to be like Daddy) he may turn to his peer group for more satisfactory models.

The traditional pattern of the boy loving his mother but fearing his father[8] is still common in the working and lower classes.[9] This is in some ways a less difficult situation than that of the middle class boy, provided the fear of the father is not overwhelming. The differences between the roles of the blue-collar mother and father are clearer, and the mother usually encourages the boy to model himself after the father or some other distinctly male figure, and in either case the occupational activities of the model are more understandable to the child.

The problem of the lower class boy is usually the most serious because the father is more likely to be absent, or there may be a series of ''fathers.'' Even when there is an adult male in the household, the mother may hold him up as an example of what to avoid doing rather than what to emulate. Thus the lower class boy is often left with no one to use as a male model except distant, glamorous figures like athletes and television characters, who offer him little help in mastering his environment or himself.[10] As a result, his strongest and most constant identifications are likely to be with members of his peer group, a situation which contributes little to the development of a value system or a personality suited to broader interaction patterns and personal growth. In sum, working class boys seem least likely to have problems in identifying with an appropriate model, which suggests that their learning of norms and values may be more convincing and thus more enduring than that of either middle or lower class boys. As grown-ups, this is the group that both figuratively and literally waves the flag.

DISCIPLINARY STYLE AND MORAL DEVELOPMENT

Discipline must be accounted a crucial variable in identification, since it demonstrates parental power and is thus a very important source of the child's ambivalent feelings toward his parents. To the extent that it embodies the subcultural values, it is also a major factor in his subcultural conditioning. On both counts the parents' disciplinary style should have a determining effect upon the child's development of conduct and character.

Another major determinant, pointed out originally by Piaget,[11] is the child's level of cognitive development, which sets limits upon his ability to make moral judgments. Kohlberg stresses the cognitive aspect of role-taking as a major means of moral development. ''Moral role-taking involves an emotional empathetic or sympathetic component, but it also involves a cognitive capacity to define situations in terms of rights and duties, in terms of reciprocity and the perspectives of other selves.''[12] It's this final perception or ability which represents the highest level of development and makes both personal guilt and moral relativism possible. Kohlberg's stages of moral development are the following:[13]

Level 1. Premoral
Type 1. Punishment and obedience orientation.
Type 2. Naive instrumental hedonism.

Level 2. Morality of Conventional Role-Conformity
Type 3. Good-boy morality of maintaining good relations, approval of others.

Type 4. Authority maintaining morality.

Level 3. Morality of Self-Accepted Moral Principles
Type 5. Morality of contract, of individual rights, and of democratically accepted law.
Type 6. Morality of individual principles of conscience.

Like other developmental sequences, this one is considered to be invariant[14] and it progresses from external constraint toward internal control. Unless the parents' disciplinary style encourages the growth of self-control, the child is likely to stall at one of the lower levels. For instance, if the parents continue to use a concrete, non-reasoning disciplinary style based upon their absolute power when the child is old enough to respond to other methods, the child may never develop past the premoral stage. In this style physical punishment and other concrete forms of discipline are not empirically associated with the formation of guilt—an important mechanism of internal control.[15]

If the parents' disciplinary style is based upon reciprocity and the legitimacy of authority, they are likely to punish for the consequences of the child's act rather than for his presumed flouting of authority. This is still a relatively concrete, rigid style but one which does take into account the rights and feelings of others. It is based on the eye-for-an-eye principle: "You broke Johnny's toy and made him cry, so now you're going to get a licking." The child exposed to this training will learn to conform to convention and to feel guilt about failure to do so, but more in the nature of mechanical reciprocity than thoughtfulness.

A disciplinary style based on reasoned explanations of norms and values, and especially on pointing out the consequences of the child's actions for others, seems the most successful in stimulating the child's capacity for moral self-judgment. Parental warmth and identification of the child with the parent have also been found to be related to guilt and internalized moral judgment.[16] Parents using this style of discipline are apt to take into account the child's intentions and other circumstantial factors, and this encourages the child to regard subcultural rules less literally and more relativistically.

Which of these three types of disciplinary style is used by the parents depends upon their own level of moral and cognitive development, and we have seen that a given style tends to reproduce in children exposed to it the level of development on which it is based. This suggests that the modal level of moral development in a social class is perpetuated over a number of generations. Let's see if this line of reasoning is supported in studies of social class variations in disciplinary style and their outcomes in children's behavior.

A number of studies have found blue-collar parents in general more likely to punish the child for the immediate consequences of his actions than middle class parents, who punish on the basis of the child's intentions.[17] In Piagetian terms these blue-collar parents are operating in terms of reciprocity and the middle class parents in terms of moral relativism. The social class comparison could also be drawn in terms of degree of stimulus-bondage—the blue-collar parents reacting to the immediate stimulus (the act itself), and the middle class parents inhibiting the impulse to react until they have explored the shadowy region underlying the child's behavior. Another explanation of the blue-collar disciplinary style emphasizes the parents' egocentric reaction to the child's behavior; they do not or cannot take his point of view or role.[18] The child is told how he should act, but no consideration is given of his understanding of these instructions or whether they are consistent with other teachings.[19] The working class mother sees her child's behavior as mysterious and beyond understanding. This is why she looks for absolute rules and authoritative guidance with which to control the child and insists upon the importance of teaching him to dichotomize morality into right and wrong.[20]

In a comparison of lower class families with "core culture"

families (lower middle plus working class), the major differences in disciplinary style were found to be in the parents' use of power.[21] The lower class parent-child relationship was psychologically closed, hierarchical, and quite rigid. Children raised in this atmosphere, always fearful of their parents' explosive anger, tended to become either bullies or submissive followers and to set up submissive-bully hierarchies in their peer groups. A Texas study points to the inconsistency of lower class discipline; the child is laughed at one day and slapped the next for the very same behavior.[22] He learns that gratifications should be seized at every opportunity, since there is no certainty they will be available later. None of this contributes toward the learning of internal control or a future orientation. Middle class children, by contrast, learn that approval and disapproval extend over longer periods, so that it is advantageous for them to think about the consequences of their actions in advance. This encourages them to take the role of the parent and become responsible for their own behavior.

The perception of parental roles also varies by social class. The working class wife sees her husband as a dominant and controlling figure,[23] and so she tends to feel that discipline is a major part of his role as father. The middle class mother emphasizes the supportive aspect of his role, with constraint being of secondary importance. The working class father tends, however, to consider all aspects of child-rearing as the mother's responsibility,[24] and therefore resents the disciplinary function thrust upon him and may project this resentment upon the child.

Family size and sex of the children affect these interpretations of parental roles in complex ways. In general, the larger the family, the more active the father is in child-rearing, except for blue-collar fathers of boys.[25] These fathers are somewhat less likely to take on disciplinary responsibilities when the family is large. On the other hand, if the blue-collar family is mainly composed of girls, fathers are very likely to play a dominant role. In middle class families the sex composition of the family has less effect than its size. But a major conclusion of the study is that "neither family size nor sex composition explains even a moderately large portion of the variation in the perceived parental behaviors . . . The effects they do have are highly contingent upon the sex and social class of the child." The sample was composed of white, Protestant seventh-graders from unbroken homes.[26] A related study by one of the same investigators using a less restricted sample found autocratic, authoritarian parents most likely to be fathers with blue-collar jobs, with a high school education or less, Catholic, and with three or more children at home. The democratic, equalitarian parents were most likely to be mothers of middle class status, with some college training, Protestant, and with only one or two children at home.[27]

It seems generally agreed that middle class mothers require children to take responsibility in the home and in their lives away from home at an earlier age than working class mothers do.[28] In their comparison of Sears, Maccoby and Levin's study with their own, Havighurst and Davis[29] found themselves in agreement that middle class children were allowed more freedom of movement away from home during the day. In the former study both classes expected good performance at school, but working class parents put more pressure on their children than middle class parents did, possibly because it was more of a problem.[30] In general, however, "the middle-class mother expects more of her child than her working-class counterpart."[31] Thus while "middle class parents are becoming increasingly permissive in responses to the child's expressed needs and desires . . . [they] have not relaxed their high levels of expectation for ultimate performance."[32]

Bronfenbrenner's research on tenth-graders[33] shows that it is the presence of rejection rather than the lack of a high degree of warmth that inhibits the development of responsibility in children of both sexes. Negligent discipline on the part of the father is associated with low responsibility in boys, but the most responsible boys were not those with the highest paternal control scores, but those with middle scores. There seems to be a critical point beyond which too much show of authority impedes rather than facilitates the development of responsibility in boys. Highest responsibility in girls' scores was also associated with paternal control scores of the middle range; the presence of strong paternal discipline, especially power-assertion, was particularly debilitating.[34] Thus it is primarily the father whose absence, affection, and—especially—authority have differential effects on the two sexes, and this effect increases at lower social levels. Here especially, weak paternal control lowers responsibility in boys, while strong paternal authority and affection lower responsibility in girls. By contrast, at the highest social level it is the mother whose discipline and instrumental and expressive activities foster the development of responsibility in boys and impede it in girls.[35]

Responsibility is, of course, an important aspect of moral development. A responsible person is able to control his own actions in accordance with his values and so is able to avoid the pangs of guilt. That is, he is internally rather than externally controlled and lives quite comfortably with his conscience. According to Gans,[36] working class people are somewhat less than comfortable with themselves; they are concerned, even preoccupied with self-control. Having little self-consciousness or detachment, they tend to project their fear of doing evil or forbidden things onto others.[37] This class tendency to project has been found in children, too, in a study in which blue-collar children were less willing than middle class children to accept the responsibility for failure and more inclined to blame it on someone else.[38]

Kohlberg has found that middle class children possess more mature moral judgment than working class children. He attributes this to the former group's more extensive social participation and responsibility and to their "sense of potential participation in the social order."[39] The last factor is represented in the social class value systems by the activity-passivity dimension and probably in the middle class disciplinary style by parents urging their children to "take part in things."

The effects of these differing social class experiences and disciplinary styles upon the development of conscience have been documented in a number of studies. Sears, Maccoby and Levin[40] found a strong conscience in the child to be most frequently associated with a preference for the use of reasoning and praise and only an occasional resort to physical punishment. For warm and loving mothers, withdrawal of love as a disciplinary technique was also associated with a strong conscience in the child.[41] These were all more characteristic of the middle than of the working class except for withdrawal of love, which showed no significant class differential.[42]

Much the same conclusions were reached in a study of seventh graders.[43] Paper-and-pencil tests and ratings by their parents, teachers and schoolmates were used to determine the strength of the child's conscience, and interviews with both children and parents (except lower class parents) provided information about disciplinary style. It was found that the parents of middle class children with weak consciences had frequently used power-assertion as a technique, while those whose children had stronger consciences had used reasoning and often pointed to the consequences of the child's actions for others. Love withdrawal was infrequently related to the moral development indices. Lower class children were generally lower on these indices than middle class children, but few significant relationships were found between lower class moral development and parental discipline as reported by the child. This could well be due to the systematic bias which was allowed to operate against the lower class respondents. No interviews of lower class parents were made. Children whom the school considered to be behavior problems and those from broken homes were excluded from the study. Finally, it proved impossible to get reports on parental discipline from about 25 percent of the sample, the loss being greatest in the lowest class portion. Under these circumstances the study can make no firm statement about lack of relationship between lower class parents' disciplinary style and the moral development of their children.

A study of 244 boys between the ages of five and fourteen used questions resembling those originally used by Piaget to measure moral development.[44] It was found that father's occupation, which was used as the indicator of social class, correlated significantly with the moral development measures, the boys of higher social status making the more mature responses by Piaget's developmental criteria. Of special interest is a group of questions on stories which depicted a conflict of norms. What was being tested was the tendency to obey rules blindly versus the tendency to make moral decisions on the basis of relative degrees of goodness. For example, one story described the accidental breaking of a window, after which the owner demands to know the name of the guilty boy in order to report him to the police. The witness (respondent), who knows the boy's name, then has to decide whether lying is a more serious offense to his conscience than getting the boy into trouble with the police. Boys whose parents had maintained strict disciplinary control were more likely to favor obeying the letter of the law in such situations. As we have seen, a rigid disciplinary style is more typical of blue-collar than of white-collar parents.

The results of the studies reviewed in this section show that the three stages of moral development characterized by externally controlled conformity, conventional conformity based on reciprocity, and moral relativism or independent moral judgment correspond roughly to the dominant disciplinary styles of the three social classes. Lower class discipline is congruent with a combination of absolutism and reciprocity. Here disciplinary style may be somewhat less influential in character development, however, than in the other classes because lower class parents give their children less time and attention[45] and the peer group plays a correspondingly larger part in the socialization process. The working class disciplinary style seems most congruent with reciprocity and conventional conformity, and that of the middle class with moral relativism or independent judgment. These disciplinary styles, which presumably reflect the developmental level of the parents, produce matching developmental levels in their children. In other words the process serves not just to produce but in fact to perpetuate the positive association between social class and moral development appearing in the studies cited.[46]

THE LOCUS OF CONTROL

We have already noted that as moral development progresses, the locus of control moves from sources external to the child into the child himself, or from constraint by adults toward moral autonomy. The basic exposition of locus of control is provided by Rotter, Seeman, and Liverant.[47] The Internal-External Scale is the device they have constructed for measuring this variable, which includes the elements of skill versus chance, one's own characteristics versus the characteristics of others, and one's own potential to control the environment versus the influence of others.[48]

The locus of control has been empirically related to the overall developmental level in children. Using a simplified and rephrased I-E Scale with normal and retarded children between the ages of six and fourteen, Bialer found that with increasing age came a significant tendency on the part of both types of children to see the locus of control as internal.[49] They also came to respond to success-failure cues rather than to concrete, hedonistic ones and to delay gratification when delay was seen to lead toward a greater reward. The retarded children did not differ qualitatively from the normal children but matured more slowly. In another study of children[50] the I-E Scale plus a new Picture Test of I-E Control, consisting of six cartoons with one projective question for each, were administered to eighty sixth and eighth graders, half of whom were black. Age was not found to be related to I-E scores, but the age span of these respondents was only about two years as compared with eight in the previous study. IQ was similarly unrelated when social class and race were controlled. However, middle class children in general were significantly more internally oriented than working and lower class children. These findings support the hypothesis of social class differentials in developmental level and also the overriding influence of the social class subcultures over the racial ones.

Another way of relating locus of control to moral development is to ask which end of the internal-external continuum is preferred by conformity-minded respondents. A study of adolescent boys' attitudes toward authority[51] used ratings based on clinical evaluations of interviews with the boys and their mothers, ratings by their teachers, and sociometric ratings. Their conformity to rules, regulations, and social standards at home, at school, and with their peers was rated on a five point scale. In general, the boys' conformity increased as socioeconomic status decreased. Based on a composite index of socioeconomic status, the sample turned out to be predominantly middle class, with only five families as low as working class. One might jump to the facile conclusion that the lower status, more conforming boys have the stronger consciences, if it were not for the fact that conventional conformity rates lower in the moral development scale than moral autonomy. The relatively superficial types of conformity investigated here can just as easily be attributed to dependence upon external control as to strong conscience. As for the higher status, non-conforming boys, the explanation that harmonizes the findings of the moral development studies with this one is that these middle class non-conformists are rebelling *against* external control in favor of their inner drive for independence.

Graves[52] believes that the ability to control time is one aspect of internal-external control. He has also linked it with social status, hypothesizing that the period of time typically taken account of in stories, personal plans, etc., would increase with increasing social status. To test this he took as subjects the entire senior class of a small Southwestern high school, consisting of 46 Anglos, 41 Spanish, 24 Navajos, and 12 Utes.[53] Six tests were used, three of which showed significant Anglo-nonAnglo differences in the direction predicted, that of longer time perspectives for Anglo than for non-Anglo students. Of these tests the I-E Scale was one of the most reliable.[54] Thus Graves demonstrated social status differences in regard to locus of control and related them to time orientation as well.

Aronfreed explains class differentials in locus of control in terms of experience, which is after all the ultimate source of and reinforcement for values. "People will have an internalized orientation to the extent that they have control over their environment and over its determination of their own behavior. They will have a more external orientation to the extent that their behavioral choices are imposed upon them by events which are outside of their control."[55] Obviously, people of higher social class exercise more power than those lower down on the ladder, and both groups know it. Their occupational situations are a good example. Middle class people have more experience with making plans and giving orders, while blue-collar people have more experience with carrying them out. The socialization patterns of the two groups reflect and perpetuate this difference. Discipline based upon reasoning prepares middle class children for a conceptualized approach to work and to people, while discipline based on power-assertion by the parents prepares blue-collar children for obedience to authority.[56] As for the effect of all this upon moral development, "The findings of almost all of the relevant surveys indicate that the shift from an external to a more internalized orientation of conscience, as the child advances in age, occurs more slowly among working class children.''[57]

TIME ORIENTATION

The factor of time orientation is closely related to locus of control, as we have seen, but it is treated separately here because it represents a separate value-dimension. The relevant literature appears under several conceptual labels: time perspective, deferred gratification, and impulse control are the major ones. There is general agreement about the relation of time orientation to developmental level. Wallace and Rabin conclude[58] after a review of 159 psychological articles that: ''The abstraction of time as continuously flowing [and] boundless both in the past and future is a relatively late acquisition of the developing individual even in the most literate society.'' Werner[59], too, has pointed to an increasing capacity for delay and planned action as one indication of developmental progress.

We have already noted the differing value orientations of the three social classes in respect to time. The connection between social class position and this factor has been suggested or implied in a variety of other contexts as well. Blue-collar people have been repeatedly described as present-oriented.[60] The cognitive styles of problem-solving in culturally deprived families have been described as ''impulsive rather than reflective,'' ''concerned with the immediate rather than the future,'' and ''disconnected rather than sequential.''[61] It has been observed in a number of community studies[62] that lower class people live in quick sequences of tension and relief, unwilling to forego pleasure for long periods or to plan action that has distant goals because of the uncertainty of their future. The working, middle, and lower-upper classes, by contrast, have long tension-relief sequences. The individual lives in regularized fashion, performing a given action only when it is the ''right time'' to do so rather than when the impulse first strikes.

Long-range plans can involve lifelong strivings toward a distant goal.

LeShan[63] attributes these class differences in time orientation to differences in disciplinary style: inconsistent and impulse-dominated discipline with immediate punishment in the lower class, and a more controlled regime in the working and middle classes. The latter leads to the formation of a character capable of renouncing immediate pleasure for the sake of future gain, while the former does not. To test these ideas LeShan asked 117 eight to ten-year-olds of blue-collar and white-collar backgrounds to write a brief story. When the stories were compared in terms of the period of time covered by the action, he found that the middle class children's stories covered a significantly longer period than those of the other children. Subsequently LeShan was accused of miscalculating his chi square value, so that his findings were supposedly non-significant.[64] More recently his data have been recalculated by Graves,[65] who dichotomized the stories into those whose action occurred in less than one day and those whose action took one day or more. The resulting chi square values for middle class versus working and lower class differences were significant between the .02 and the .01 level, the stories of blue-collar children being significantly shorter in time span.

A widely noted study of "deferred gratification" used a representative sample of 2,500 high school students.[66] Since the sample was representative of youngsters in school rather than of all teenagers, the lower class was undoubtedly underrepresented. The respondents were stratified on the basis of father's occupation and a subjective rating of their class status. Twenty-eight questions were asked, and the predicted class-related pattern of deferred gratification emerged. Unfortunately several of the questions were such that objective conditions of life such as income and size of family could determine the answers. One question sought to determine the intensity of the respondent's pursuit of education, and another asked whether the parents had saved money to help the child get a good start in life. These questions may be assessing the reality level on which the family operates. A third asked respondents to check which of twelve occupations they considered "not good enough" for their life work, a question which would seem to test level of aspiration or concern with status rather than willingness to defer gratification. Two more questions seem to test closeness of parental supervision rather than impulse-rejection, or external versus internal control: one on the parents demonstrating strong ideas as to what the youngster's friends should be like, and one on being well-mannered and obedient. Questions on sexual gratification had to be worded vaguely in deference to the high school administrators' wishes and produced no meaningful results. Generally, the evidence collected in this study is of questionable value.

Another study whose results are questionable investigated the willingness to defer the gratification of five adolescent needs: affiliation, aggression, consumption, independence, and sex, using four items for each need.[67] Correlations between the five scales were low and suggested two rather than one deferred gratification pattern. One represented the tendency to defer material needs (consumption and economic independence), the other the tendency to defer interpersonal needs (affiliation, aggression and sex). Social status was measured by a 7-point scale based on five objective criteria; the lower class was scarcely represented. The scale taken as a whole was significantly related to academic achievement and occupational aspiration when social status and intelligence were held constant, and of course social status was also significantly related to these two variables. But except for deferment of economic independence, no evidence was found of a positive correlation between social status and deferred gratification. As in the case of the previous study, however, serious questions can be raised about some of the items.

Four items are said to have been included to test willingness to defer gratification of each of the five needs. Yet only sixteen of the twenty are presented in the report, and two of these are criticized by the author himself. Five more seem challengeable:

1 "I have certain standards which my friends must meet." (Affiliation) This sounds more like a measure of universalism versus particularism than of deferred gratification. If a new acquaintance does not help the respondent to gratify his affiliation needs, he can gratify them elsewhere. Few normal persons defer making friends for long periods because of their standards.

2 "Teenagers have to be careful about the behavior of the crowd they go with." (Affiliation) One would expect almost every high school student to agree with this out of his own observations, and 90 percent did. Therefore the gratification of finding a "safe" crowd does not have to be deferred.

3 "Since school started last fall, how many of your arguments have led to fights?" (Aggression) There are two problems here. One is that fighting is assumed to be more gratifying than arguing or name-calling for boys of all social classes. The other is the failure to realize that a person who does not want to fight may still respond to a punch by returning it in order to protect himself.

4 "From what you have experienced, who would you say usually wins in settling arguments?" (Aggression) Ninety-one percent chose "the smart and tactful." This choice clearly denies the assumption that fighting is more gratifying than arguing. It is hard to see any connection with deferred gratification.

5 "How much education do you definitely plan to get?" (Economic Independence) The answer to this for high school juniors and seniors is surely as strongly related to family income as to willingness to defer gratification. Further, Beilin[68] has made the point that college attendance may in fact represent gratification for boys from lower social classes.

And this may be true for many boys from higher classes as well, especially those who picture college in terms of freedom from parental supervision and from the pressures of a job.

If these items plus those questioned by the investigator himself are dropped from the scale, only nine of the sixteen remain. For these reasons the non-significant results of this study are no more useful than the significant results of the previously described study. A plea of *nolo* must be made in respect to social class differences in time orientation, but perhaps more careful investigation will produce better evidence in the future.

A TYPOLOGY OF CHARACTER DEVELOPMENT

Out of the child's identification with his parents—or the lack of it—his disciplinary treatment, and the degree of control he experiences over himself and his environment, he acquires a set of values and attitudes which constitute his moral character. A set of values and attitudes which is too weak or too inconsistent to withstand the exigencies of the moment renders the individual stimulus-bound, the creature of every event and impulse. Not only does he lack self-direction or internal control; he lacks a destination or future orientation as well. In sum, he has a poorly developed or weak moral character. At the opposite end of the developmental continuum is the individual with a relatively consistent set of values and attitudes, one whose priorities are established on the basis of a distant goal, possibly evolving and forever unattainable. This goal provides not only aspiration for the future but direction for the present, a direction determined by internal and therefore relatively flexible factors rather than by external factors. The internally controlled, future oriented person has a strong character structure.

Affective and cognitive experiences vary from one social class to another, as studies have shown. Therefore it is reasonable to expect that different types of character are found at different class levels, and, more specifically, that the modal level of character development should increase with each step in the social class hierarchy. This inferred relationship receives support in an intensive longitudinal study of 36 children in the community which has been variously called Elmtown, Prairietown and Jonesville.[69] In this study the level of moral development is used as the basis on which to build the following set of character types.

Character Type	*Developmental Period*
Amoral	Infancy
Expedient	Early Childhood
Conforming	Later Childhood
Irrational-Conscientious	
Rational-Altruistic	Adolescence and Adulthood

The relation of this typology to Freud's oral, anal, oedipal and genital stages and to Piaget's stages of moral development is obvious.[70]

These types are thought of as the stages through which the individual normally passes on his way to full maturity. But because most people stall somewhere short of full maturity, adults as well as children can be found representing all of these character types. The Amorals have no conscience; as adults they may become "psychopathic personalities" if basically hostile, or charming ne'er-do-wells if gregarious.[71] They are subject to neither internal nor external control. The Expedients yield to external control, but in its absence they do as they please. They have no internalized moral principles—no conscience.[72] The Conformists learn how to behave by habit and obey the rules unthinkingly and unquestioningly. This type probably corresponds to Riesman's "tradition-directed" type, which is discussed in detail in Chapter 5. There are no degrees of morality and no necessary overall consistency; behavior may be specific to the occasion.[73]

This differs from the Expedient approach in that here social conformity is accepted as good for its own sake.[74] The Irrational-Conscientious type behaves in conformity to a code he has internalized completely. He has a rigid, blind superego, with no awareness that rules are made by man and intended to serve human purposes.[75] The Rational-Altruist has a stable set of moral principles to go by, but he assesses each new action and its effects for the welfare of others as well as himself. He is fully socialized, doing what is right because he wants to, not merely because he is supposed to.[76] He sees himself and others realistically, is emotionally mature and well-adjusted.[77]

From Amoral to Rational-Altruistic an evolutionary development can be traced. There is:

1 Increasing ego strength,
2 Increasing strength of conscience,
3 Increasing ability to love,
4 Gradual maturing of the impulse life into desires which are inherently socialized.[78]

Peck and Havighurst found that these tendencies or the lack of them grew out of the affective experiences of infancy and later childhood. The Amorals had experienced chaotic inconsistency and almost no mutual trust or affection. Some parents of Amorals were autocratic and severely punishing; the rest were lenient and rather laissez-faire. The Expedients had had a good deal of lenient, indiscriminate freedom from parents who tended to approve of them in a rather off-hand inconsistent way. An occasional family was highly consistent, severely controlling and mistrustful. Conformists came from consistent autocratic families with severe punishment. Some had experienced trust and love, some had not. A subgroup came from backgrounds much like that of the Amorals but were characterized by a "beaten-down anxiety to comply." The Irrational-Conscientious subjects all came from very severe families with average to high consistency. Otherwise they differed somewhat. Rational-Altruists had consistent, strongly trustful and loving, highly democratic, and lenient rearing.[79]

Although the investigators found no direct connection between character type and social class, except possibly at the lower class level,[80] they reported that:

1 character maturity was highly correlated with school grades,[81]
2 and that the highest sociometric ratings went to Rational-Altruists.[82]

Both of these indicators are related to social class in many other studies, and things equal to the same things are equal to each other. Perhaps a larger sample than thirty six would have produced more definitive results.

In any event there are strong similarities between some of these child-rearing descriptions and the various social class disciplinary styles described earlier. On the basis of their childhood affective experiences the Amorals and Expedients would seem most likely to be found in the lower class. The Conformists and Irrational-Conscientious seem to have been brought up by a type of discipline most likely to be found in the working class and perhaps in the lower middle class as well. The Rational-Altruists' type of character would most likely be found at the upper middle class level, judging by their affective experiences. And so this study leans in the direction of supporting the association of social class position with level of moral development and the major role of parental disciplinary style in effecting it.

CONCLUSION

The child's learning the subculture of his social class has been treated as a primarily affective experience because it involves learning what he ought to do and how he ought to feel. He learns these moralistic lessons by imitation, identification and conditioning. Modelling, the affective process basic to both imitation and identification, is more difficult for boys than for girls. It is especially difficult for lower class boys and least difficult for working class boys. Discipline, the major means by which the parents condition the child, is an affective technique but one whose characteristics are determined by the cognitive level on which the parents operate. If they view the subcultural norms and values concretely, their disciplinary style tends to be stimulus-bound, rigidly concentrated on how closely the child's behavior matches the norm. If they view them more abstractly, their style is more flexible and responsive to the child's needs rather than to his acts.

Since the level of cognitive development has been shown to be closely associated with social class level, disciplinary style should show the same relationship, and this is borne out by a number of studies. Middle class parental behavior is likely to be helpful, relatively permissive, verbal, playful, empathetic and individualized. Working class parents are generally less verbal, less playful, more authoritative, more repressive and rigid. They are also likely to make more distinctions between the rearing of sons and of daughters. Lower class parents are the most likely to use physical punishment and other forms of power-assertion, to be impulsive and therefore inconsistent, to spend little time with their children, and to raise girls and boys differently.

Also borne out empirically is the further inference that the child's cognitive and moral development does not as a general rule progress beyond the highest level reached by his models and preceptors. This suggests that the modal developmental level of a social class can be perpetuated over long periods of time. In the next chapter we shall see that the selective processes of upward and downward mobility also contribute to this stability.

A useful way of categorizing the outcome of the child's subcultural indoctrination is in terms of the resultant locus of control. The individual's moral development may be looked at as a progression from external toward internal control, from subjection to the will of others toward self-determination, or from a passive stance toward an active one. Studies support the prediction that at any given age the higher the individual's social status, the farther he is likely to have progressed along the road to internal control. Time orientation is one aspect of control over oneself and one's environment. The externally controlled person presumably concerns himself first with the present and secondarily with past experiences. The future is of little concern since it will not be of his making. The internally controlled person may be expected to concern himself mainly with the future toward which he is building. The present then becomes a tool for reaching future goals, and the past has value only for its applicability to the present and future. These two different value-orientations toward time have frequently been said to characterize the lower and the middle class respectively, the working class taking a position somewhere between them. However, the evidence for all of this is sparse, and more carefully designed studies will have to be carried out before the postulated relationships can be affirmed.

The typology of moral character worked out by Peck and Havighurst summarizes the consequences for personality of the varieties of affective experiences involved in learning the social class mores. It supports the thesis that the stages of moral development are linked to the three social class levels in the same systematic way that the stages of cognitive development were found to be. It also foreshadows the personality typologies that are described in Chapter 5.

4

Where and How
to Belong

Social Class Differences

in

Interaction Patterns

Up to this point we have been concerned with the differential learnings of children growing up in the three social classes. Now we turn our attention to their parents in order to discover what adult experiences support social class differences in child-rearing and home environment, and how these differences have managed to persist in the face of rapidly changing social conditions.

The stability and continuity of any subculture require forms of social organization and styles of interaction which embody its norms and values. This means that we should expect to find social class differences in the types of groups which parents (and any adults, for that matter) belong to and in the social relations found within them. From the enormous range of groups within our society the individual chooses particular ones mainly on a developmental basis, if our theory is correct. That is, a group's attractiveness depends upon the degree to which its style of interaction—the ways its members behave toward one another—is congruent with the prospective member's developmental level. If it is highly congruent he can fully belong, and the personality structure formed in childhood is continuously reinforced in adulthood by his association with like-minded people. Since his child-rearing techniques have also been selected on the basis of his developmental level they, too, receive support from his experiences in groups, not just those within the family but those well beyond it. And in the social class as a whole, as the personality development of large numbers of its members stabilizes at a certain level, the class subculture stabilizes accordingly and thus is able to endure.

The discussion begins in the heart of the family, where one would expect to find the greatest degree of intimacy and therefore the strongest influence upon personality. The pattern, like so many others we have examined, turns out to be determined by social class.

PRIMARY GROUP INTERACTION PATTERNS

Husband and Wife

In the two lower classes the marriage relationship is based upon sex role segregation. "Husband and wife have a clear differentiation of tasks and a considerable number of separate interests and activities. They have a clearly defined division of labor into male tasks and female tasks. They expect to have different leisure pursuits, and the husband has his friends . . . the wife hers."[1] Even when people visit in a private home, the men are likely to cluster in one room and the women in another, with little or no interaction between the sexes.[2] This is a very different pattern from that found in the middle class, where few distinctions are made between the proper behavior of males and females and where the marital relationship can thus be a closer and more companionable one.[3]

One of the outcomes of the sex role segregation pattern in the lower classes is that marriage partners have less conversation with each other than middle class couples do.[4] Apparently this social class difference is qualitative as well as quantitative. An experimental study using a laboratory task has found middle class husbands and wives to have much more accurate communication than lower class partners.[5] Another study presented middle and working class families (couples plus one child) with a motoric, nonverbal problem.[6] Although this type of problem does not discriminate against lower class people, it was the middle class families who solved it most efficiently, and they did so by means of superior communication skills. The previous chapters suggest that these middle class skills can be accounted for in several ways: by the verbal skills acquired in childhood, by the possession of a formal language to supplement the public one, by the high value placed on cognitive activities by the middle class subculture, by the universalistic orientation, and by girls and boys being brought up in much the same manner, which eliminates one barrier to communication. So far as the marriage itself is concerned, their greater communication skills make it possible for middle class marriage partners to have a better understanding of each other than those of the lower class.

The sex role segregation found in the lower classes has a dampening effect also upon specifically sexual attitudes and behavior.[7] Several studies have shown that working and lower class women have much more conservative attitudes than women in higher classes and diminished sexual satisfaction as well.[8] Men have much more aggressive attitudes and tend to see women in terms of their sexual accessibility or inaccessibility.[9] Extramarital relations are considered quite understandable for the husband but are strongly disapproved of for the wife. This Victorian definition of marital sex roles is shared by both husbands and wives and is transmitted to their children. Boys are overtly and covertly encouraged to learn about sex by experience, while girls are kept in prudish ignorance insofar as possible.[10]

Satisfaction with the marital sex relationship seems to vary with the degree of sex role segregation, which as we have seen varies with social class. The class variable operative here may well be education. In one study sexual satisfaction was much more closely related to educational differences than to differences in income or occupation.[11] No doubt this is due in part to the effect education and information have upon marital communication. It is probably also related to the effect of education upon family planning, another factor in sexual satisfaction. In one study[12] about 80 percent of the couples in which the wife had at least some high school education had used contraceptives or planned to do so. The comparable figure for couples in which the wife had less than a high school education was 60 percent. Over 75 percent of the more educated women had begun to use contraceptives before their third pregnancy, as compared with a little over 50 percent in the less educated group. Some of this differential is probably due to differences in understanding of the reproductive process. If one does not understand this, it is hard to regard a contraceptive as anything other than magic and impossible to choose intelligently between various devices or methods. Rainwater found that less than half of the working class women he interviewed, and only about one quarter of those in the lower class, understood the functions of sperm and ovum.[13] More than half of the men in both classes gave incomplete or inadequate explanations of conception, such as "the male lays the egg." These encourage the use of the condom and other inefficient contraceptive techniques and thus lead to a higher rate of unintended pregnancy. This is a prime example of powerlessness based upon a low level of cognitive skills. It also provides a functional explanation for the minimal sex education given to children.

If sexual satisfaction varies with social class, this should be reflected in differential divorce and desertion rates, and in fact it has been for at least twenty-five years. One frequently cited early finding was that working class marriages were broken twice as often as those in the middle classes and that lower class marriages were the least stable of any.[14] A later investigator[15] constructed an index of marital instability based upon 1960 Census data and applied it to lower, middle, and upper income groups. Their indices were twenty-three, ten, and six, respectively. Reviewing studies of divorce, Goode[16] has concluded that "there is a rough *inverse* correlation between class position and rate of divorce. . . . this is not a matter of simple economic causation, but is the resultant of the family patterns at different strata." However, recent changes in family patterns may be producing changes in the relation between social class and marital instability.

In recent years there has been a drift away from sex role segregation among working class people. A more equalitarian and communicative type of marital relationship is developing,[17] a change attributable not only to thirty years of post-war prosperity and improved economic security but also to the increased spatial mobility of families.[18] Moving from one community to another or even from one neighborhood to another breaks up the network of kinship and friendship ties which has maintained the continuity and stability of the working class subculture. The result, however unintentional, is an increased interest and involvement in the nuclear family and increased intimacy in the marital relationship.[19]

The traditionalistic tendency among blue-collar people to raise boys and girls differently can be viewed as a consequence of sex role segregation in the parents' marital relationship and as an antecedent of it in the marriages of the next generation. If working class marriages continue to move in the direction of equalitarianism, strong sex differentiation in the rearing of their children may be expected to diminish accordingly.

The Extended Family Versus Friends and Neighbors

A number of studies agree that except for those who move away from the hometown, American working class people's interests and activities center around the extended family, which is a fairly large and co-operative group.[20] For example, a study of suburban working class people in California[21] found that 47 percent of them visited relatives often, and only 19 percent reported visiting them rarely. Another study found that half of the people seen most frequently by working class wives were relatives, as compared with 20 percent in the middle class.[22] Still another study, using area sampling, reported that 41 percent of working class and 59 percent of lower class respondents saw relatives more frequently than anyone else.[23] The comparable figures for middle class people were 16 percent for upper middle and 21 percent for lower middle. One factor which helps to explain these differences is the differential accessibility of relatives; blue-collar families are more likely to have relatives living nearby than middle class families are.[24]

Friends are an alternative source of sociability and help. Since everyone's time is limited, the more time people spend with relatives, the less they have to spend with friends. Therefore we would expect to find fewer and fewer friendships as investigations descend the social class ladder. This is borne out by the finding that only about 11 percent of upper middle class people and 18 percent of working and lower middle class people report no close friends, compared with almost one third (30 percent) of those in the lower class.[25]

The most obvious places to make friends are in the neighborhood, on the job, and in a voluntary organization. In one working class sample 34 percent of the respondents reported having a mere nodding acquaintance with their closest neighbors, while only 19 percent reported being very friendly with them.[26] Wives, of course, are more involved with their neighbors than husbands: in one study 62 percent visited them often or occasionally, and most of the wives who did not were employed.[27] In general, however, neighborhood visiting is discouraged by working class people in favor of visiting with relatives.[28] Lower class wives spend more time than those of any other class in visiting neighbors on an average weekday, even though lower class couples visit least with neighbors in the evenings—again because relatives are preferred.[29]

So far as blue-collar men are concerned, in a recent study of over 600 only about 10 percent of them perceived their important primary relations as taking place at work; the rest preferred to experience them elsewhere.[30] This is in line with earlier findings that the work and home sectors of blue-collar experience are kept separate. Workmates are not generally invited to the home and are seldom seen outside of work.[31] This is a very different pattern from that of the middle class person, whose career orientation encourages him to make friends on the job because they can be useful as well as enjoyable. Friends serving as role models can facilitate personality development as well as occupational advancement.

In studies covering the last thirty or more years children's friendships show a strong and consistent tendency to follow social class lines both in the neighborhood and in the classroom.[32] This, after all, is where children meet one another, and both residential areas and school districts show a good deal of social class segregation. When choices are made outside of the chooser's own class, they are likely to be made in a higher social class, but this may be due as much to admiration of the higher class child's behavior and competence as to perception of his higher social status.[33]

SECONDARY GROUP INTERACTION PATTERNS

Patterns of adult voluntary participation in the neighborhood and in the larger community have remained remarkably constant in the past thirty years and probably for an indefinite period before that. The positive relationship between social class and number of memberships is the basic pattern noted in all studies.[34] Considering the importance of voluntary associations in offering individuals a means of coping actively with their environment by advancing their political, economic, and social interests,[35] it's ironic that those who need advancement most do not use their franchise of membership.

An area study of Detroit found 27 percent of the total population to be without formal group memberships;[36] 17 percent more held only church membership, while 50 percent of those with any membership whatever held only one. The proportion holding memberships increased directly with social class. In 1951 60 percent of the working class men in New Haven and 75 percent of their women and children did not belong to any formal organizations.[37] For the remainder who did, many of the memberships were inactive, especially those in unions, military, fraternal, and ethnic organizations. Among New Haven's lower class, another study found about 75 percent of the families completely isolated from community organizations except for nominal church membership.[38] A few belonged to unions but were not active in them.

A study of United Automobile Workers in Detroit found that 9 percent did not even think to mention their union membership when asked what organizations they belonged to.[39] Church membership was the most common one held (51 percent). After that came lodges and other fraternal organizations (17 percent), and a scattering of veterans' organizations (8 percent), social and church-related clubs (7 percent), and so on. The striking thing about these figures is the size of the interval between types of memberships: from 91 percent (union) to 51 percent (church), to 17 percent to 8 percent. Leaving out the union and church, which are not voluntary associations in the same sense that the rest are, the number of memberships is small indeed. The reason that it is smaller than the number in some other blue-collar studies is because this sample included blacks, women, and a large proportion of semi- or unskilled workers, all of whom are even less inclined to be "joiners" than white working class men are.

Class differences are found not only in the number of member-ships held but also in the type of organization joined. While middle class people prefer political and service organizations and others representing broad interests,[40] blue-collar people are more likely to favor social and fraternal organizations and unions.[41] However, the clubs and societies arousing the most working class inteiest are those that approximate the informal organization in structure and function.[42] For example, New Haven men who joined athletic clubs tended to be active members. These were small local associa-tions, some of them organized around a neighborhood bar clique. Individually the clubs were ephemeral, but their tradition was well established in the local culture. To join more formal associations, an individual would have to inhibit his suspicion and hostility toward people outside of his primary groups and enter into rather impersonal relationships with them. This is not easy for most blue-collar people, whose model for all social relationships is the family. It is no accident that those who do join voluntary associa-tions choose fraternal, social-recreational and church-related ones, where primary relations are an important objective and where there is little connection with the larger community.[43]

Most of the studies note that not only do white-collar people belong to more organizations, but they attend more frequently and are more likely to hold office than blue-collar people.[44] This is probably related to the fact that working class participation is based more upon necessity (e.g., in unions) and less on feelings of civic interest and/or responsibility, desire for status, and related considerations.[45] The same thing can be said of working-class wives.[46] They do not easily identify with purposes that go beyond those of face-to-face groups; even participation in the PTA is looked upon as a way of finding out how one's children are doing rather than as a means of improving the schools. Differences in education are probably an important factor in these class differences in participation patterns.[47] As for lower class people, they generally belong to few if any organizations and are the least likely to attend meetings. In fact, the differences in participation between lower class and working class people are greater than those between working class and middle class people.[48]

The formal organization with which most blue-collar men have the most contact is the company they work for. It is not unreasonable to expect this to be a highly meaningful affiliation in view of the time spent in it and the high salience of its reward. Dubin has shown that among the 600 industrial workers he studied three out of every five indicated that their company was indeed the most significant organization in their lives compared to the church, lodge or club on a number of points.[49] This did not mean, however, that they necessarily liked the company more. In fact three out of four indicated that work and the workplace were *not* central life interests.[50] It appears that the blue-collar worker has developed a strong sense of attachment to the physical and other obvious features of his work, i.e., its concrete aspects, without the corresponding sense of social or professional commitment to it that many middle class workers feel.[51] Another study asked workers if they would continue to work after inheriting a rather large sum of money.[52] Of the middle class workers 86 percent said they would continue to work, compared with 79 percent of working class and only 22 percent of lower class workers. As in the case of the number of memberships held and also the degree of participation, the major split comes between the two lower classes rather than at the blue-collar/white-collar line.

The blue-collar pattern of generalized disinterest in clubs, churches, and occupational organizations is observable, too, in relation to government. Erbe has found eighteen studies that show a positive association between socioeconomic status and political participation covering the last thirty to forty years.[53] In his own sampling of three communities he found the same pattern. His political participation measure included informal political discussions, attempts to influence public officials, participation in campaigns, financial contributions, and frequency of voting in the past four years. The SES Index included education, family income, and occupational prestige; its three levels probably correspond respectively to upper middle class and above, lower middle plus working class, and lower class.

TABLE 6
Political Participation by Socioeconomic Status[1]

| | *Political Participation:* | | |
Socioeconomic Status Index	*High*	*Medium*	*Low*
High (N = 202)	47%	43%	11%
Medium (N = 187)	19%	55%	27%
Low (N = 204)	11%	49%	40%

[1] William Erbe, "Social Involvement and Political Activity: A Replication and Elaboration," *American Sociological Review* 29(1964): Table 1.

Even that most powerful of political attractions, a presidential election, does not motivate much more than half of the low income group to vote, although well over three quarters of the upper income group does, according to Census figures.[54] The general rule seems to be that the lower their social class status, the less likely people are to vote or to be politically active in other ways.[55] Since this matches their behavior in respect to other formal organizations, it is not surprising to find that organizational involvement is as good a predictor of the degree of political participation as socioeconomic status is.[56] The importance of alienation in this equation is derivative, according to Erbe's statistical analysis; it emerges as an effect of low status and low involvement in organizations rather than as a cause.

TABLE 7
Voter Participation, by Income,
in the Presidential Election of 1968[1]

Family Income Per Year	Percentage of Eligibles Voting
Under $3000	54
$3000-$5000	58
$5000-$15,000	72
$15,000 and over	84

[1] Richard M. Scammon and Ben J. Wattenberg, *The Real Majority* (New York: Coward-McCann, 1970), p. 54.

Let us summarize the social class differences found in the various kinds of interaction patterns. Within the marital relationship sex role segregation is the outstanding characteristic of the blue-collar pattern. It is especially prominent in the lower class, where both partners have a negative attitude toward the wife's sexuality that gets in the way of their sexual satisfaction. Lack of education is probably a factor here, as it is in ineffective family planning. Sex role segregation in other aspects of married life, too, e.g., in the division of labor and leisure activities, serves to hinder communication and intimacy. In part, sex role segregation depends upon having closely knit extended family networks which separate the interaction patterns of husband and wife. In a portion of the working class the advent of a more equalitarian marital relationship and a stronger focus on the nuclear family are beginning to weaken sex role segregation.

In general, working and lower class people prefer to confine their primary group relationships to the nuclear and extended families. Middle class people also use the extended family as an important source of help and sociability, but they prefer to interact more with friends than with relatives.

Class differences in secondary group interaction patterns have been extremely stable for a long period of time. Number of memberships, frequency of attendance, and office-holding are all positively related to social class. A considerable number of blue-collar people belong to no voluntary associations at all, especially in the lower class. Church affiliation appears to be the commonest type of blue-collar membership, but this does not necessarily imply attendance or participation.

The type of organization belonged to also differentiates between blue- and white-collar groups—the former favoring those that most resemble informal groups in structure and function, and the latter those with much broader aims and interests. The blue-collar worker appears to join organizations primarily through constraint of some kind, as in the case of the union and the church, but he apparently feels no similar constraint in relation to civic or political affairs. His sociability needs are taken care of within the extended family and peer group, so he has no need to "meet people," and using voluntary associations as a step up the status ladder is not a working class practice nor one which fits into the working class subculture.

Lower class people represent the extreme of the blue-collar participation patterns, but there is a greater difference between the lower class and the working class in this respect than between the working class and the lower middle class. However, it is important to note that these are quantitative differences only: number of memberships, frequency of attendance, and number of offices held. The more crucial difference, the qualitative one, lies between the blue- and white-collar groups and involves the differential functions of memberships, the type of organizations joined, and so on.

To the extent that the interaction patterns of the blue-collar groups reinforce the primary group style and reject secondary relationships, they operate to keep the modal developmental level lower than that of the white-collar group. Primary relations are more present than future oriented, less rational and less actively oriented toward the environment (because they turn inward), and more particularistic than universalistic. Important and enjoyable though all of these qualities are, they cannot by themselves enable people to develop to full potential. To put it formally, primary relations are a necessary but not a sufficient condition for the attainment of psychological maturity.

SOCIAL CLASS MEMBERSHIP: STABILITY VERSUS MOBILITY

It could be said that our social class system is open in spite of itself, since most of its functions foster stability and impede mobility. The biggest loophole is the reliance upon occupation as the major placement device, for a person can change his occupation more readily than he can his family background or his education. But although the American dream of "getting ahead" is shared by most people, i.e., by both the working and middle classes, the boundary-maintaining forces producing stability still have to be overriden before the individual can move up in the system. The same thing is true for anyone moving down. The ideal of "getting ahead" is itself a good example of a boundary-maintaining mechanism. It makes the uppermost boundary of a class more permeable and at the same time strengthens the lower boundary against downward mobility.

For our purposes the most noteworthy mechanism is the social stratification of groups, a factor which encourages stability by keeping the interactions of members for the most part confined within their own class boundaries. Interaction within one's own social class means interacting with people who have the same subcultural values and thus reinforcing them. This structural press toward both personal and subcultural stability operates throughout the life cycle of the individual.

The young child is taught and treated according to the values of his parents, which are the values of their social class plus some verbalizations of societal ideals. His playmates are typically the children of neighbors, relatives, or personal friends of his parents. Thus they are usually of the same social class, a few being a stratum or two higher or lower within that class, and so they share his family's values and interaction patterns. In fact if they do not, contact with them is very likely to be discouraged. The effect of this preferential interaction is that the child is exposed to a virtually undiluted social class subculture during his early years. When he enters school, he tends to remain in the same subcultural milieu because school districting reflects residential stratification patterns. The middle class child will find the teacher's values and style of interaction congruent to his own, but for the blue-collar child these are likely to clash with his earlier learnings. If his own value system is supported by a classroom peer group, he will find it easy to "turn her off" and discount the worth of school.

Children's behavior toward voluntary associations follows that of adults in type of organization chosen and extent of participation. A few blue-collar children, perhaps upwardly mobile, join middle class organizations.[57] Their preferred associational pattern, however, is membership in a sex-segregated informal peer group.[58] The sex-segregated peer group is a phenomenon of middle class childhood, too. The differences are that middle class children also become involved in formal organizations and that by middle adolescence the middle class peer groups come to include both sexes.

The tendency for peer grouping to reflect social class grouping increases progressively from middle class to working class to lower class, and this tendency is increasingly supported at each subsequent level by ethnic, religious, and racial boundary-maintenance practices. Middle class peer groups are less exclusive than those of the other two classes probably because of the greater tolerance of variation and the wider variety of strata within this social class. Nevertheless, the maintenance of the social class subculture is an important function of the peer group at all levels of society.

When he has finished his formal education, the individual enters an occupation which delimits the social and physical conditions under which he will live. Once on the job, his closest associates are usually people of his own social class. His associations with people of other classes are likely to be governed by the distancing mechanisms of the formal organization. During his leisure time the same conditions hold. His closest associates are people of his own social class, whether in primary or secondary groups. He marries someone who shares the same social class subculture or is willing to learn it. In the blue-collar life cycle it is only during this brief period of courtship and the early days of marriage that the peer group loses its hold on the individual. Then the tendency is for lower class people to return to their old peer groups and for working class people to extend theirs to include the new in-laws and a few friends of each spouse.[59] Thus there is a good deal of structural support for the maintenance of class subcultures at every stage of life except (in the case of the two blue-collar groups) in school.

While the interactions of the individual are being circumscribed by social class patterning, his subculture is being built into his personality. Virtually all of the experiences of the growing child are colored not only by the cultural biases of his society, but more particularly by those of his social class. And each class-biased learning acts as a filtering device on subsequent experiences, allowing information which is congruent with earlier learnings to be assimilated and screening out incongruous or dissonant information.[60] In this way, the integrity of the social class subculture is supported from the "inside" by the moral and cognitive characteristics it inculcates in the individual just as it is from the "outside" by the structural press of its interaction patterns.

If the internal and external factors which support the maintenance of social class boundaries worked perfectly, we would have a caste system in the United States. Actually social stability, as measured by sons' occupations being at the same prestige and income level as their fathers', seems to characterize a little less than half of all urban American families, so that social mobility is by a slim margin the prevailing pattern. The rates of stability and mobility vary predictably by social class. Upper middle class families are the most likely to have experienced upward mobility, while lower middle and working class families are the most likely to be stable. Downward mobility is found most frequently among lower class men.[61] A good deal of the upward mobility in the middle classes is attributable to the opportunity factor: i.e., to the continuing trend toward a higher proportion of white-collar jobs in the occupational structure.

While the incidence and direction of mobility are largely attributable to economic factors, it is maintained here that the *selection* of mobiles is attributable to developmental factors. Our proposition has been stated in terms of *modal* tendencies: *modal* developmental level is positively associated with social class level. It follows that in each social class a considerable number of personalities may be expected to be more highly developed than the modal type and a considerable number less so. It is reasonable to conclude that those more highly developed than the majority in their social class are more likely to be upwardly mobile, since their developmental level gives them the skills and attitudes necessary for success in the next highest class or stratum. For this very reason they may feel somewhat out of place in their social class or stratum of origin, so that the "push" of psychological discomfort is added to the "pull" of economic and social opportunity.

The same kind of explanation fits the case of downward mobility. Personalities which are underdeveloped relative to others in the same social class will not only be at a disadvantage in the job market but will also suffer the discomfort that goes with comparative ineptitude. These are the personalities most likely to drift down to a lower social level where they may find themselves more comfortable on the job and in their social relationships—provided they do not define downward mobility as failure.

A certain amount of socialization into the subculture of the new social class is probably necessary for all upwardly mobile persons, even those who are relatively highly developed. This is best accomplished by identifying with a member of the class who is perceived as being a superlative example of whatever needs to be learned. For maximum usefulness the model should be available for frequent face-to-face interaction.[62] Whether or not the resulting relationship is a permanent one does not matter sociologically so long as it lasts long enough for the upwardly mobile person to supply those deficiencies in his development which interfere with his fitting into his new class status. Probably, then, upward mobility always involves some further personality development.

Downward mobility by contrast does not, because the individual is moving into a social milieu characterized on the whole by a lower developmental level, a level on which he is presumably already operating for the most part. To the extent that he is not, moving downward will involve a certain retrenchment of the self, as activities become more concrete and as social relations become less complex and more demanding of conformity. While upward mobility involves dynamic personality change, downward mobility would seem to involve stasis or regression.

While these selective mobility processes have important consequences for individual personalities, they do not seriously affect the stratification system. In society—as in any other organization—what matters is not which individuals perform various functions, but whether there are enough qualified people to perform them. If it is generally the more highly developed personalities who move up in the occupational structure and the less well developed personalities who move down, then the correlation between social class and modal developmental level will be maintained or even increased. In this way both upward and downward mobility function to support the stability of the social class structure and its associated gradation of personality development.

CONCLUSION

When the interaction patterns of the three classes are examined, they are found to embody their respective value systems. Working and lower class husband-wife relationships are characterized by a traditionalistic, stereotyped sex role segregation which impedes marital communication and satisfaction. The blue-collar preference for interaction with the extended family rather than with friends also reflects traditionalistic attitudes, while the tendency of white-collar people to seek out other congenial associates in addition to relatives is an acting-out of their belief in individuality. The tendency to belong to and participate in formal organizations is similarly associated with social class. Lower class people appear to distrust and reject them. Working class people are willing to join an organization in which membership offers a benefit and/or non-membership a penalty, but they are not likely to be active participants. The blue-collar groups' preference for primary relationships is presumed to have a limiting effect upon personality development. The white-collar groups by contrast not only join more organizations but participate more actively in them, demonstrating their manipulative and universalistic orientations. Middle class interaction patterns may be considered to show greater maturity than those of the other two groups in that they surpass those of the latter both in quantity and in quality.

The boundaries of a social class are maintained by a structural press toward confining the interactions of its members within their own social class, where their class value orientations are constantly reinforced. This press begins with parental choice of playmates and is continued by class-segregated interaction patterns in the neighborhood, the school, and the workplace. It is supported within the individual by his class-biased learning experiences, which tend to make him feel more comfortable with members of his own social class (who are on the same general developmental level) than with others. Those whose experiences have given them a higher or a lower developmental level than others in their class are candidates for upward or downward mobility, subject of course to economic conditions.

Upward mobility probably involves even for personalities of above-average development for their original social class some degree of further personality development. In the same way downward mobility must often involve some personality change, but here it would involve regression rather than growth. The effect of these processes so far as the stratification system is concerned is a stabilizing one, since they maintain the homogeneity of the subculture at each level and group personalities in such a way that within each class most people are more comfortable with themselves and with their associates than they would be in any other class. Thus both upward and downward mobility function to maintain the stability of the social class system and its associated hierarchy of developmental levels.

5

The Stratification of Personality Types

Social Class Differences

in

Modal Personality

When the values of a social class are consistently implemented in its interaction patterns, the personality it typically produces should embody these distinctive subcultural features. This is its modal personality. Rather than constructing the modal personality type of each class out of the materials collected thus far, we are going to risk our pile on other people's ready-made types. We shall do so by trying to fit some existing typologies of personality to the values and child-rearing patterns found to be typical of our three social classes.

This will be of necessity a matching and piecing operation, since the typologies were produced for different purposes than ours and since the social background materials are not complete in every case. A more irksome problem is the fact that the typologies have been conceptualized in terms of ideal types, the most extreme exemplars of certain personality dimensions, while we are working with the concept of modal personality, the type most commonly found at a particular social class level and therefore a middle-of-the-road rather than an extreme type. Figure 2 illustrates this discrepancy between 'types of types' which we shall have to keep in mind. Messy though our procedure may be, it at least has the virtue of utilizing a new group of constructs which have been independently arrived at.

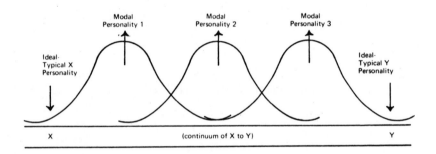

Figure 2. Discrepancy Between Ideal-Typical and
Social Class Modal Personality Types

If the values and child-rearing patterns associated with the personality typologies match the social class patterning already described, then the types may serve as approximations of the modal personalities we are searching for. All of the typologies conceive of personality in developmental terms, but each approaches it differently. The first is based on cognitive functioning, the second on attitudes derived from affective experiences, and the third on the referents of conformity. Finally a synthesis of types at each developmental level is attempted along with their social class placement to see what the social class modal personalities look like.

A COGNITIVE TYPOLOGY

The reasons for emphasizing the role of cognition over that of affect in personality development, even though they are closely linked, were given in Chapter 1. It was pointed out that degree of stimulus-bondage seems to be the general factor underlying the developmental continuum, a factor which depends primarily upon the level of cognitive functioning. To be stimulus-bound is to be confined to a concrete perception of and response to the stimulus, and freedom from the concrete aspects of the stimulus depends upon the ability to perceive and respond to it in an abstract way. At the same time the cognitive processing of information through the individual's frames of reference or conceptions, be they concrete or abstract, must inevitably include an affective evaluation of the information based upon the individual's needs and other feeling states.[1]

Setting aside the affective components insofar as possible, Harvey, Hunt and Schroder have worked out a set of personality types based upon the level of cognitive functioning. In the simplest terms, the personality which functions concretistically sees situations and objects as undifferentiated totalities and so can react only to their grossest, most immediate characteristics; the stimulus dominates perception and response. The personality which functions abstractly analyzes a situation or object into its component parts and is able to manipulate them mentally. In so doing, he discovers their interdependence and comes to understand the working of the articulated whole. This enables him not only to deal with it effectively at the moment but also to predict with some accuracy how it will work in the future. In other words the highly developed personality dominates the stimulus.[2]

The evidence in Chapter 2 of a positive relation between social class and level of cognitive functioning suggests that the modal personality of the lower class should be located within the concrete end of the cognitive continuum—though not at the very end—that

TABLE 8
Concretistic Cognitive Characteristics and the Blue-Collar Value-Dimensions

To attribute causality to external factors, partly because wishes and beliefs are seen as coextensive with and inherent in the external world.[1] To have difficulty in shifting one's perspective as a situation changes.[2]	Passivity
To be categorical and absolutistic in one's thinking because one's concepts are based on minimal dimensions and alternatives.[3] To be ritualistic, especially in new situations.[4] To be negativistic and resistant to suggestion, except when the suggestion comes from an authoritative source symbolic of power and security.[5]	Traditionalism
To find it difficult or impossible to assume a mental set willfully and consciously. To be unable to explain why one does things or why others do, which limits the ability to take the role of the other.[6]	Particularism
To seek out and prefer familiar and reassuring objects, both animate and inanimate, especially in new situations.[7]	Primary Group Orientation
To have difficulty in planning ahead, which requires an "as if" mental set.[8]	Present Time Orientation

[1] O. J. Harvey, David E. Hunt, and Harold M. Schroder, *Conceptual Systems and Personality Organization* (New York: Wiley & Sons, 1961), pp. 38-9.

[2] Ibid., pp. 30-1.
[3] Ibid., pp. 36-7.
[4] Ibid., pp. 43-6.
[5] Ibid., pp. 42-3.
[6] Ibid., pp. 29-30.
[7] Ibid., p. 45.
[8] Ibid., p. 34.

the middle class type should be within the abstract end—though not at the very end—and that the working class type should be somewhere in between. Illustrating this in Figure 2, if X stands for concreteness and Y for abstractness, the type 1 modal personality will be that of the lower class, type 2 that of the working class, and type 3 that of the middle class.

What sort of evidence can be produced to support this schema? In Table 8 the dimensions of the blue-collar value system are matched with the characteristics of Harvey, Hunt, and Schroder's concretistic personality type. While the correspondence is evident, the description of the concretistic personality consistently overstates the tendencies found in the working class. Because an ideal type is being depicted, it more accurately describes tendencies of the social class nearest the end of the continuum, the lower class. In fact it is highly reminiscent of the description of the lower class survivors of the Arkansas tornado (Chapter 2). In other words, this personality description supports the position that the lower class modal personality is more concretistic than the working class type.

The personality which has reached the abstract level of cognitive development is characterized by possessing the very abilities that are lacking or poorly developed in the concretistic personality: internal control, flexible perspectives, and so on. And these abilities form the cognitive foundation of the middle class value-dimensions: activity, rationalism, universalism, and future time orientation. The goodness of fit between these polar personality types and the value-dimensions of the white-collar and blue-collar groups encourages further examination of the cognitive typology.

While maintaining the notion of a universal developmental continuum, Harvey, Hunt and Schroder do not conceive of it as progressing in a straight line through gradually unfolding stages. Rather they see it as occurring in a series of cycles, each of which is initiated by the child's having to face a new developmental problem and reverting temporarily to a concretistic mode of functioning in order to do so. Within a given stage or cycle the process of dealing with this problem is a dialectical one, with thesis, or recognition and acceptance of a factor, generating the recognition and acceptance of its opposite or antithesis. The differentiations or finer discriminations which grow out of these pulls in opposite directions eventually produce a new integration of the components, a synthesis on a higher level.[3] Here the dialectical process is repeated, the individual utilizing his new perceptions and discriminations to reassess his environment.

Not all personalities manage to complete the full set of cycles or stages. Development may suffer an arrest in any stage. In Harvey, Hunt and Schroder's thinking this may occur in two different ways. First, when the environment or "training conditions" present the theme or thesis of a stage in positive terms and its antithesis in negative, threatening terms, the developing individual naturally cleaves to the positive or rewarding pole rather than to the punishing pole and so does not progress beyond it. Second, when both thesis and antithesis are presented in simultaneously positive and negative terms, as at once rewarding and punishing, a state of conflict is set up in the individual, causing him to recoil in confusion and so fail to progress out of the stage.[4]

The notion of developmental arrest should not be taken to imply, however, that the personality remains forever that of a child or that no change can take place thereafter in the problem area which brought about the arrest. Rather it means that the subsequent formulation of conceptions *in that area* cannot go beyond the level of concreteness or abstractness intrinsic to the stage in which the arrest occurred.[5] So far as the developmental level of the whole personality is concerned, the more complete the arrest, i.e., the more closed the conceptual system* to the further differentiations or discriminations necessary for progress, the more its level of

*The term "conceptual system" refers to a set of interrelated conceptions or frames of reference pertaining to a particular area, such as the self.

functioning tends to be generalized to other areas. Therefore some personalities came to be quite evenly developed in all areas, with most of their conceptions or conceptual systems operating on the same level of cognitive functioning. Others, whose closure in the area of arrest has been less complete, will show a more uneven developmental profile, utilizing in the arrested area(s) conceptions typical of an early stage of development and in other areas more sophisticated conceptions.[6]

Let us now examine in detail the "training conditions" which Harvey, Hunt and Schroder posit as producing each successive level of arrested development and see how closely these approximate the child-rearing practices of the three social classes as described in Chapter 3.

Stage I: Unilateral Dependence

The term "unilateral" refers to the fact that the child's dependence is involuntary, resting on his inability to differentiate adequately between internal and external stimuli. Because he obeys his parents' rules blindly, his behavior is often ritualistic. Before the child can progress out of unilateral dependence, he must differentiate himself from the outside world. He must learn to discriminate between various factors involved in external control: rules and their purposes, animate and inanimate sources of control, and so on. When this is accomplished, he has taken the first step toward conscious control over his own behavior.[7]

Stage I is primarily concerned with dominance/submission or hierarchical status, in-group/out-group differentiations, and right and wrong. The discriminations developed are characterized by inflexibility because they depend on absolutistic criteria, so submissiveness is the response style not only to authoritative persons but to other forms of external control as well.[8] All of these match the blue-collar value system, particularly the working class version. The style of child-rearing which is said to lead to arrested development in Stage I is autocratic and highly consistent. (A positive presentation of the dependence pole; a negative presentation of the independence pole.)

Absolutistic criteria are used in judging the child's behavior, but the required behaviors are well within his ability to perform and are consistently rewarded.[9] This sounds very much like a conscientious working class upbringing. It also resembles the upbringing of the inner-directed, a type described later in this chapter. An arrest in the transitional phase to Stage II is associated with heavier parental demands, often beyond the child's level of ability. Training is consistent but highly controlling, with lavish extrinsic rewards for success and punishment for failure. (Both poles presented as rewarding and punishing.) A rigid, authoritarian, anxious personality is produced by these conditions.[10] This child-rearing pattern looks like an extremist form of the working class pattern. It could also be found in middle class families which suffer from status-anxiety as a result of recent mobility either up or down.

Stage II: Negative Independence

The thesis of this stage is resistance to external control. In its early, concretistic phases it takes such forms as stubbornness and resentment of interference. If the child's imperious self-assertion is not arbitrarily put down by parental power-assertion, he will eventually come to admit and even to enjoy a measure of dependence upon his parents. These opposing tendencies begin to be integrated as the child learns to discriminate between those areas in which he may usefully claim independence and those in which he may still profit from the support and guidance of others. (Both alternatives are presented positively, so development is encouraged rather than arrested.) Once he accomplishes this, he is able to handle problems of dependence in more relativistic, more abstract terms.[11]

In Stage II, the individual is concerned with freeing himself from autocratic and absolutistic controls. When development is arrested here by parental resistance, the child's resentment of his powerlessness turns into hostility and aggression. Arrest in Stage II is associated with the same child-rearing methods used in Stage I but applied and rewarded inconsistently. There is less affection and good will in the parent-child relationship, and many of the parent's demands seem autocratic because they are beyond the child's ability.[12] This is a fair description of one type of lower class child-rearing and of a reactive type of working class child-rearing. The value system most congruent with hostility and aggression is that of the lower class, so children of this class experiencing this kind of upbringing will find their home environment continuous with that of the neighborhood. When working class children become stalled in a state of hostile aggressiveness, their adult performances as workers and family members will be so far below working class standards as to force them down into the lower class. There they will rapidly become acculturated because the value system is more supportive of their angry feelings.

Having just explored two avenues to membership in the lower class, we may as well complete the survey by examining a third. This is an upbringing characterized by parental neglect and indifference, conditions presumed to have the same effect on personality as an autocratic, inconsistent upbringing.[13] However, neglect and indifference would not carry the child as far as Stage II. They would probably stall his development just short of or on the threshold of Stage I, since he could never have learned to depend trustingly upon his parents. This type of childhood experience might occur in any social class, but the pressures of lower class life make it more likely to occur here than at other class levels. It would be interesting to know what proportion of membership in the lower class is attributable to each of these environments: an inconsistent autocratic training by lower class parents, the same by working class parents with eventual downward mobility for their offspring, and neglectful indifference.

Arrested development at the point of transition from Stage II to Stage III is brought about by what is popularly called permissiveness: lack of direction in the child-rearing process and indiscriminate approval of all that the child does.[14] In this situation the child can learn instrumental behavior only by imitation or by accident. Besides failing to learn adequate instrumental skills, the child fails to learn to handle his own frustrations and readily falls prey to sulks and tantrums. So long as he is with his parents this presents no problems, for both sides understand their roles and play them consistently. The parents are submissive and the child dominant.

His troubles begin when he tries to interact with others who will not tolerate his behavior. His response to their rejection takes the form of hostility and aggression.[15] While this is not the typical childhood experience in the middle classes, it is unlikely to be found very often in the others, since it is usually based upon a theoretical approach to child-rearing. Children brought up in this way, like others whose development is arrested in Stage II, are candidates for lower class status, but much of this potential downward mobility is probably averted by the middle class strategem of defining problem behavior as neurotic or emotionally disturbed. This ensures special treatment for the individual, softening the environmental demands upon him and legitimizing his claims on the tolerance and sympathy of others.

Stage III: Conditional Dependence and Mutuality

The child who reaches Stage III is now able to keep himself sufficiently in the background to understand other people's points of view, and this makes mutual relationships possible. In the early phases he may be almost compulsively sociable and cooperative. His openness also leads to a more empirical approach to his own experience, and this makes it possible for him to "try on" various views of himself, other people and events without being threatened by the ambiguity or lack of closure. He finds that his experimental attitude enables him to discover how best to please other people, and their rewards reinforce the tendency. Out of all this the child constructs a firmer model of what he wants to be and therefore of what standards he should set for himself. He moves from a consideration of the concrete data, so to speak, i.e., other people's conceptions of what he should be and how he can reach their goals, to an abstracted conception of his ideal self. In doing so he frees himself to a considerable extent from external control.[16] Through such experiences the individual is able not only to develop his own individuality but also to respect that of others. Social relationships now can be cooperative and competitive, rather than grossly dominant or submissive.[17]

This rational yet sensitive, generalizing yet individualizing orientation is clearly congruent with the middle class value system. The child-rearing techniques that are said to produce it include the following:

1 rewarding the child for instrumental behavior, so that the ends are no longer the only consideration and "failure" may be viewed as a way station on the road to success;
2 using emotional supports not only as a reward but also as a teaching device in the form of direct help and acting as a model;
3 encouraging free give-and-take, so that the child begins to develop his own criteria rather than relying on externally given ones.[18]

Development is arrested in Stage III when emotional response and support become more important to the child than information.[19]

Arrest during the transition between Stages III and IV is brought about by the premature loading of responsibility upon the child, even when this is done in a non-controlling way.[20] This sounds much like a technique that would be used by busy, ambitious middle class parents. It produces conflict in the child between his desire to behave independently and the fear that in doing so he will not be able to meet other people's standards.

Stage IV: Interdependence

In the stage of full maturity the more extreme forms of mutuality and independence are blended into a comfortable state of interdependence. The individual is no longer dependent upon the constant support and approval of others, but neither does he hold himself aloof from their needs and opinions. His self and the other conceptual systems through which he interprets experience have been integrated and equilibrated. The learning of skills and information has provided him with the means of solving problems. Both his world view and his problem-solving ability reflect his abstract mode of functioning, which combines a consistent approach to the environment with an openness to alternative views and new information. This personality type is the most resistant to stress because its reality-based self-confidence leads it to define fewer situations as threatening, and because when a situation is so defined, the mature personality has more resources at his disposal for dealing with it.

The upbringing necessary to produce the Stage IV level of maturity is characterized by maximum openness to both thesis and antithesis at each preceding stage. To accomplish this the environment must be so arranged that problems are kept within the child's ability to solve, making protectiveness unnecessary. Since particular solutions are not insisted upon, he is free to develop alternative ones and also his own criteria for choosing between them. Rewards are given for instrumental behavior, but they are neither personal nor extrinsic. Rather they are based upon a colleague relationship.[21] Through these methods the child becomes independent of others' support and of ready-made frames of reference while still able to enjoy collaborative effort.

The middle class value system and child-rearing pattern matches the Stage IV upbringing almost as well as it matches that of Stage III. That is, the children of typical middle class parents have the potential of developing personalities of either Stage III or IV. The emphasis here is on potential, because many other factors besides values and child-rearing practices affect child development. Two are especially influential, the school system and voluntary associations, since the middle class child spends such a large proportion of his time in them.

Schools serving middle class residential areas are most likely to emphasize cooperation and competition, Stage III characteristics. The individualized problem-setting and encouragement of alternative solutions needed to produce Stage IV are difficult to provide in the ordinary classroom setting, and when attempted these techniques easily degenerate into Stage II non-directive permissiveness. The developmental effect of recreational and "character-building" associations is probably quite similar, their own measure of success being the frequency of Stage III functioning. If the middle class child spends approximately one third of his waking hours the year round in school and voluntary associations, and probably somewhat less than one third with his parents, the developmental implications of organized activities outside of the home are apparent. The remaining third or more of the child's time is spent with his peer group, where the level of functioning is not likely to be higher than it is at home or in organized activities. For the middle class child, then, the developmental ceiling is set at Stage III by the community, and his home training—if this is of the Stage IV type—offers the only chance to break through it. Even this opportunity dwindles with age, as the child spends more and more time outside of the home.

Table 11, found later in this chapter, summarizes the social class implications of the Harvey, Hunt and Schroder typology. The other three typologies are presented there in the same fashion, so that analogies between them are apparent.

AN AFFECTIVE TYPOLOGY

The next set of types is labelled ''affective'' because it is based upon psychoanalytic theory and highlights the effects of emotional experiences upon perception, cognition, and social relationships. This time the ideal type at the X or stimulus-bound end of the scale (Figure 2) is the well-known ''authoritarian personality,'' a type characterized by conventionalism, authoritarian submission, admiration of power and toughness, superstition and stereotypy, destructiveness and cynicism, and projectivity of sexual and other impulses.[22] The ''non-authoritarian'' is, of course, its diametric opposite. Frenkel-Brunswik, who was part of the original research team, noted in a subsequent publication the generalized immaturity of authoritarians.[23] Since many of their qualities are normal in developing children, the development of authoritarians would seem to have been arrested in one of the early stages.

If authoritarianism is associated with a relatively low level of development, then its characteristics should show some correspondence to the blue-collar value system, just as those of the concretistic personality do. In a general way they do correspond, with the usual discrepancy between ideal and modal types. Most of the authoritarian characteristics clearly exemplify traditionalism and passivity, but the connections with particularism, primary group orientation and present time orientation are less clear. Rokeach[24] has emphasized the authoritarians' concrete, rigid cognitive style which may underlie these; for example, their strong in-group/out-group dichotomizing may underlie the primary group orientation. The factors of power and toughness, destructiveness and cynicism, and projectivity, however, point directly to the lower class variant of the blue-collar value system. Thus the ideal type of authoritarian probably matches the lower class value system better than that of the working class, though it has a recognizable affinity with the latter. And if the lower class modal personality—the type which most completely embodies the lower class value system—is the more authoritarian, then it follows that it is also less mature than that of the working class. Some empirical validation of the connection between social class status and authoritarianism is provided by Lehmann.[25] Administering Rokeach's Dogmatism Scale to over 2,700 freshman entering Michigan State University, he found that the degree of stereotypic beliefs, traditional value orientation and dogmatism were inversely related to social class. Probably only a few of these respondents came from lower class homes, but the study supports the logic of our position. At any rate a contrary finding would have given us pause.

The childhood experiences reported by high authoritarians have been found to include the following:

—rigid discipline with conditional affection;
—clearly defined roles of dominance and submission, with faithful execution of duties and obligations rather than free-flowing affection;
—forced repression of aggression toward authority coupled with contempt for weakness;
—exaggeration of sex-linked personality attributes as compensation for repressed hostility toward parents;
—narrow development of the ego associated with general lack of insight and rigidity of defenses;
—status-concern arising from the externalization of values;
—development of a superego mainly directed toward the punishment, condemnation, and exclusion of others.[26]

Most of these are more congruent with descriptions of working class than of lower class child-rearing, perhaps because they are based on empirical data rather than on ideal-type formulations. They also match Harvey, Hunt and Schroder's account of developmental arrest in Stages I and II rather nicely.

The final item on the list is amplified in the following statement, which supports the discussion of conscience development in Chapter 3 and by extension the social class location of authoritarianism:

> [Authoritarians], due apparently to lack of genuine identification with the parents, do not succeed in making the important developmental step from mere 'social anxiety' to real conscience. Fear of punishment by external authorities rather than [internal control by] self-chosen and ego-assimilated principles continues to be the primary determinant of their behavior.[27]

Empirical support for this interpretation is available in the significant correlation between high externality on the James-Phares Scale of Internal-External Control and high scores on the F scale of authoritarianism.[28] Authoritarianism appears to be at least in part a defense against feelings of lack of control over one's self and one's world.

Christie seems to have been the first to suggest that the F scale might be tapping different springs of behavior in the lower classes than it does in the middle classes, a point argued at length by Lipset[29] and later by others.[30] Blue-collar respondents are exposed in their everyday life to the realities that are represented by the F scale items.[31] Thus they must be expected to react differently to them than the more sheltered middle class respondents do. All of these critics conclude that authoritarian attitudes are the normal outcome of the customary experiences and values of blue-collar people rather than a pathological symptom, as the psychiatrically oriented theorists would have us believe.

Stewart and Hoult,[32] who are also dissatisfied with the psychoanalytic interpretation of authoritarianism, suggest that social-psychological factors account more adequately for social class differences in authoritarianism. They review eleven studies which show that authoritarianism is especially prevalent among: 1) the less educated, 2) the aged, 3) rural dwellers, 4) members of disadvantaged minorities, 5) members of more dogmatic religious organizations, 6) members of lower socio-economic strata, 7) social isolates, and 8) members of authoritarian families. It can be seen at once that the category of lower class subsumes more of the others than the category of authoritarian families does. The psychoanalytic focus on childhood experiences within the family is too narrow to explain such a range. Blacks, for example, do not typically experience an authoritarian upbringing, nor do lower class people, who are probably more likely to suffer from indifferent than from restrictive child-rearing. The factor common to all of these categories, Stewart and Hoult maintain, is that of limited contacts and points of view. They suggest that the degree of authoritarianism is negatively correlated with the number of roles the individual has mastered. This explanation emphasizes the cognitive foundations of and limitations upon personality and pushes affective factors into the background.

Interestingly enough it is one of the co-authors of *The Authoritarian Personality*, Daniel Levinson, who softens the extremist aspects of this type to the point where it begins to fit the working class subculture. The "traditional personality" which he and a colleague describe is a non-pathological personality type, since it is the embodiment of a certain 'family ideology' or set of values rather than a result of distorted relationships within the family. It is more heuristic sociologically in its implication that this type represents continuity with an older historical pattern. Its congruence with the Stewart-Hoult thesis is worth noting, too: both point to the sociocultural limitations on personality development.

The major characteristics of the traditional personality are taken directly from *The Authoritarian Personality*. They are:

—conventionalism;
—authoritarian submission;
—exaggerated masculinity and femininity;

—extreme emphasis on discipline;
—moralistic rejection of impulse life;
—anti-intraception or a generalized rejection of intense
   feelings.[33]

It should be noted that Levinson has dropped the authoritarian factors of superstition and stereotypy, power and toughness, destructiveness and cynicism. He gives no explanation for his selection or rejection of factors, but those dropped seem much more descriptive of the lower than of the working class. We are left, then, with a fair approximation to lower class personality (or one type of it) in the authoritarian type and an equally fair approximation to that of the working class in the traditional type.

Before leaving the cognitive and affective typologies, let us pull them together by looking at a few empirically confirmed links between .them. What common ground exists between the authoritarian-traditional and the concretistic personality types? One common area has already been noted in the positive correlation between feeling externally controlled and having authoritarian attitudes.[34] The belief in external control is the first concretistic characteristic listed in Table 8.

In a study of perceptual preferences, Barron[35] found that the preference for a complex alternative rather than a simple one was positively related to personal tempo, verbal fluency, impulsiveness, expansiveness, originality, good taste, and artistic expression. It was negatively related to rigidity, repression of impulse, politico-economic conservatism, subservience to authority, ethnocentrism, and social conformity. The complexity/simplicity dimension investigated here seems congruent with the second characteristic of the concretistic pattern shown in Table 8.

Intolerance of ambiguity, a prime indicator of authoritarianism, is congruent with both the second and the fourth characteristics. It is associated with strength of hostility, a power orientation, externalization or projection, and rigid stereotyping.[36] Severe repression of fear, weakness, and other unacceptable tendencies leads to narrowness and rigidity of consciousness which sets the stage for the generalized development of intolerance of ambiguity.

In their description of the cognitive organization of high-scoring authoritarians, Adorno and his associates include, in addition to intolerance of ambiguity, a rigid set and outlook with preconceived categorizations inaccessible to new experience.[37] (The second characteristic in Table 8.) Despite their negativity and resistance to suggestion, however, authoritarians and concretistic personalities are gullible because of their submission to authority, lack of independence, and lack of critical judgment.[38] Rainwater[39] has explained the working class wife's suggestibility in the same way. Rokeach[40] has found ethnocentrics, those scoring high on the E scale of authoritarianism, to be both more rigid and more concrete in experimental problem-solving situations than more cosmopolitan subjects. The relation of intelligence to the various levels of cognitive organization did not account for these results.

Scodel and Mussen[41] characterize authoritarians as rigid, extraceptive, conforming, lacking in insight into other people, and dependent upon belonging to the in-group—practically a restatement of blue-collar characteristics. In their experimental procedure which paired high scorers on the F scale with low scorers and then asked them to predict each other's responses to F scale and MMPI items, they found that the high scorers were less accurate in their perceptions than their low scoring partners. This corresponds to the third characteristic of concretistic functioning in Table 8.

All of this empirical evidence serves to cross-validate our first two typologies and to confirm the notion that they are both aspects of the same developmental continuum.

A HISTORICAL TYPOLOGY

David Riesman turns away from the psychological emphasis

upon individual experience to point up some of the long-range historical trends which affect it. His typology is based upon the "mode of conformity" inculcated into its members by Western society at various stages in its development.[42] The oldest personality type, which was the modal type in the Middle Ages, he calls "tradition-directed."[43] It is described in terms applicable not only to members of medieval society but also to members of modern underdeveloped societies: i.e., it is the product of a *Gemeinschaft*, folk or peasant society. The tradition-directed person is one whose conformity and modes of behavior are patterned by his ascribed statuses—group memberships which have been thrust upon him, like those of age-grade, clan and caste.

The type produced in response to the changes of the Renaissance, the Reformation and ultimately industrialization, the "inner-directed" personality, was the invention of the emerging middle class.[44] This is a more adaptable type because its behavior is not so rigidly pre-programmed. While tradition is still important to the inner-directed person, he presents it to his children in a more generalized way. Thus the inner-directed child grows up having more leeway for choice and innovation. The increasing complexity of society in the last 500 years has provided a wider and wider range of choices, both in respect to behavior and in respect to traditions themselves, and the constant necessity for choice has encouraged heightened self-consciousness and individualization.

The most modern type, which is seen as "emerging in very recent years in the upper middle class of our larger cities," Riesman calls "other-directed."[45] This is a still more adaptable type, one which is oriented toward making quick shifts not only of behaviors but even of goals, in response to signals from his contemporaries. Motivationally the other-directed personality is dominated by an insatiable need for his contemporaries' approval and by the rather diffuse anxiety which accompanies this need.[46]

Riesman is not primarily concerned with the social class location of his personality types except as they indicate changes in the dominant culture. For our purposes it is necessary to establish this connection and, as before, we shall do so by trying to match the characteristics of each type with the social class value systems. He does not give us enough information on differential child-rearing techniques to use them as a class placement device.

Riesman describes the tradition-directed person as one who

> hardly thinks of himself as an individual. Still less does it occur to him that he might shape his own destiny in terms of personal, lifelong goals or that the destiny of his children might be separate from that of the family group. He is not sufficiently separated psychologically from himself (or, therefore, sufficiently close to himself), his family or group to think in these terms.[47]

In other words he is primary group oriented, passive rather than active, externally controlled by custom and tradition, and particularistic. And if he cannot shape his own destiny nor that of his children, he must be oriented more to the present and past than to the future. After allowance has been made for the extremism inherent in ideal-type conceptualizations, the closeness and comprehensiveness of this match places the American variety of the tradition-directed personality squarely within the working class.

Lower class personality appears to be characterized by cynicism, hostility, and the expectation of deprivation. Its major goal is immediate, exciting, concrete action, although many lower class women hold out the goals of stability and security to their children.[48] It seems to embody a broken-down, defeated version of working class values. As such it cannot be considered tradition-directed but rather is anomic in relation to working class traditionalism. That the lower class falls off the end of the scale both in terms of values and in terms of historical personality type poignantly illuminates its perennial outcast position.

According to Riesman, the inner-directed and other-directed types are predominantly found in the "old" and the "new" middle classes respectively.[49] The old middle class is composed of entrepreneurial and professional people, as compared to the new public-relations-oriented bureaucrats and salaried employees. The congruence of inner-direction with the middle class value system is clear in Riesman's description of inner-directed people. "[They have] a feeling of control over their own lives and see their children also as individuals with careers to make."[50] Here are internal control, activity, individualism, and future orientation. They are also said to have a rational or scientific cast of thought and individualistic attitudes.[51] Here are rationality and once more individualism. They are enterprising and primarily concerned with the problems of the material environment,[52] a perfect statement of old middle class "activity."

Other-directed people, however, are described as primarily concerned with the actions and wishes of others.[53] They have moved from the older form of activity, a productive manipulating of the environment, to the newer one of manipulating people,[54] including themselves. They are more oriented toward consuming than producing, and other personalities are "the greatest of all consumables."[55] While the old middle class manipulates the environment in an abstract manner, i.e., through conceptual operations, the new middle class manipulation of people is even more abstract.

This difference in level of abstraction applies both to means and to ends. The older personality type uses machines and paperwork systems to gain material goods and the power that goes with them. The newer personality type uses attitudinal sensitivity and personal address to achieve popularity and influence. While material goods represent a goal to the inner-directed person, they represent a means to the other-directed, a means of demonstrating taste and acquiring influence.[56] Since rationality is not as useful in manipulating people as in manipulating things, it is dethroned or at least forced to take on as consort a non-rational and anti-traditional sensitivity to people. The result is a refined and expanded form of particularism which is linked with a cosmopolitan universalism, a combination less paradoxical than it seems.

This new form of particularism is one based upon a universalistic ethic rather than parochial loyalties. The heightened ability to take the role of the other, which grows in part from the cognitive ability to abstract the basic principles underlying the behavior of others, leads to an expansion of the primary group orientation to cover more and more people. In the process, particularistic sympathies are aroused for groups with whom the other-directed person may never have any personal contact, such as the Vietnamese and ghetto dwellers. The result is that "the other-directed person is, in a sense, at home everywhere and nowhere, capable of a rapid if sometimes superficial intimacy with and response to everyone."[57] This apt description of the watered-down quality of the primary group orientation among other-directed people points also to the decline of the rugged individualism that characterized the inner-directed. "The peer-group becomes the measure of all things; the individual has few defenses the group cannot batter down."[58]

From what has been said about the other value-dimensions, it is apparent that the other-directed person is not oriented toward the future in the compulsive manner of the inner-directed person, who is quite capable of ignoring the conditions of the present for long periods of time for the sake of future rewards. Nevertheless the other-directed person must take some account of the future in order to keep abreast of the constant changes in a modern society, but it is the immediate rather than the distant future that is most important. This makes the present more crucial as the time when trends must be recognized and choices adjusted to them.

When the inferred value orientations of the other-directed are summarized and compared with those of the old middle class, which is predominantly inner-directed, it becomes apparent that a

TABLE 9
A Comparison of Middle Class Value Systems

Inner-directed or *Rationalistic Value System*	*Other-directed or* *Neo-humanistic Variant*[1]
—Activity; manipulation of the physical environment	—Less activity; manipulation of the social environment
—Rationalism	—Sensitivity to others by means of intuition as well as or rather than by knowledge
—Universalism	—Universalism fused with particularism to extend it to a broader field
—Individualism	—A flexible form of self-consciousness tied to a vastly expanded primary group orientation
—Future orientation	—Present orientation with constant reference to the immediate future

[1] Renaissance "humanism" meant the achievement of self-realization through reason, a critical spirit, and an appreciation of history, and so is applicable to the rationalistic value system. The term "neo-humanism" refers to the attempt to go beyond it by incorporating it with other elements.

new value system is emerging. While the old middle class rationalistic value system is the polar opposite of the working class value system, that of the emerging neo-humanistic looks like an attempt to synthesize the other two in the Hegelian sense. It is concerned with those not personally known as well as with intimates, with reason as well as feeling, with the present as well as the future, with people as well as things.

The developmental implications of Riesman's historical personality types are apparent in their trend toward increasing self-consciousness[59] and the concomitantly growing ability to take the role of the other. It is hard if not impossible for the tradition-directed personality to think of himself as changing or as taking on new roles. While the inner-directed personality has more choices, they are limited by the rigidity of his character. But the other-directed personality's heightened self-consciousness enables him to maintain indefinitely an openness to the influence of others and therefore an openness to change.

One important reason for these differences is the fact that the socialization of the earlier historical types was carried on for the most part by the parents and their surrogates, while the socialization of the other-directed is placed in the hands of the peer group from the earliest years.* Other-directed children are taught that the most important signals and cues come from their peers and that the parents' approval depends in large part upon the approval of the peer group.[60] Therefore one must work on one's self throughout life. The self-consciousness of the other-directed person turns away from the differentness of full individualization and towards the flexibility and protective coloring essential for belonging to a greatly expanded, heterogeneous primary group.

At the upper end of his scale of development Riesman places the

---

*All modern children spend a good deal of time with their peers, but this does not seem to be as deliberately arranged and encouraged by other parents as it is by the other-directed.

"autonomous" personality, one capable of conforming to the social norms but free to choose whether or not to do so.[61] "His autonomy depends . . . upon the success of his effort to recognize and respect his own feelings, his own potentialities, his own limitations. . . . This [heightened] self-consciousness is not a quantitative matter, but in part an awareness of the problem of self-consciousness itself, an achievement of a higher order of abstraction."[62] Apparently the difference between the autonomous type and the other-directed is that the latter is self-conscious in an anxious way because he has "no clear core of self"[63] but a constantly changing one, whereas the autonomous personality knows himself and understands what this knowledge involves. In the first case conformity is based upon needing the approval of others, and in the second upon 'being true to oneself.' The autonomous personality, then, is the more mature on both counts: his self-consciousness rests upon a more abstract base, and his self is less subject to external control. Since Riesman feels that autonomy will develop, if it develops at all, out of other-direction,[64] he evidently locates it in the new middle class. To extrapolate from his thesis, the middle class continues to be the seed-bed of characterological change in Western society, as it has been since the Middle Ages, and it will continue to produce increasingly mature personality types. (This is discussed in detail in the final chapter.)

A DEVELOPMENTAL SYNTHESIS

Erik Erikson's epigenetic stages of the life cycle and the processes by which the individual moves through them[65] provide the most comprehensive way of looking at development. They relate the cognitive to the affective functions, and the stage-by-stage projection of these into social structure suggests a historico-developmental theory broader than Riesman's. Although Erikson stops short of a personality typology, the consequences of arrests in development are implicit in his description of the stages. For all of these reasons his theory is treated here as a developmental synthesis which subsumes the other theories presented in this chapter.

Erikson presents a series of developmental stages, each of which has a positive and a negative component (cf. Harvey, Hunt and Schroder's thesis and antithesis). The "growth-crisis" of each stage is the problem of integrating or synthesizing these, since a proper balance between them is essential to normal development.[66] However, in Erikson's thought their desirability is not equally weighted; for optimal development the positive pole must predominate. The learnings of each stage then function as expectancies and interpretive conceptions upon experiences in subsequent stages.[67] Furthermore, Erikson does not believe that incomplete or imperfect learnings cannot be compensated for in later years nor that the adequate solution of developmental problems in early stages insures the individual against the recurrence of these problems in subsequent stages.[68] In his view the door is never closed on the individual's growth through problem-solving, and this explains why he is not concerned with arrests in development or with personality typing. The justification for deriving a typology from his work is the fact that patterning of the experiences of individuals, in particular by the social class subculture, may help or hinder their personality development in patterned ways. In other words, we take the step from potentiality to probability—from Erikson's formulation of the *ideal* individual's development to a consideration of the *typical* individual's development at specific social class levels in our society.

Presumably personality development can be constricted, whether temporarily or permanently, in any one of Erikson's stages. And as each stage consists of a positive and a negative aspect or phase, the arrest takes place either in the one or in the other. Since level of development gives a distinctive stamp to personality, each level of arrest would have to produce a different

TABLE 10
Erikson's Stages, Their Cognitive and Affective Tasks, and Related Social Structures[1]

Erikson's Stages	Growth Crises	Cognitive Tasks	Affective Tasks[2]	Related Social Structures
I	Trust and Mistrust	attention observation inspection	hope (drive)	organized faith
II	Autonomy and Shame-doubt	affirmation negation exclusion postponement	will (control)	law and order
III	Initiative and Guilt	investigation contemplation scrutiny reflection	purpose (direction)	moral law
IV	Industry and Inferiority	representation transcription paraphrase metaphorical thought	skill (method)	technology
V	Identity and Identity Diffusion	intuition generalization insight individuation	devotion (fidelity)	ideology
VI	Intimacy and Isolation	paradox enigma	love (affiliation)	organized cooperation and competition
VII	Generativity and Self-Absorption	tolerance perception	care (production)	education and tradition
VIII	Integrity and Despair	"ultimate concern"	wisdom (renunciation)	literature and philosophy

[1] Richard M. Jones, *Fantasy and Feeling in Education* (New York: New York University Press, 1968), pp. 130-1.
[2] The affective task of each stage is listed in its subjective aspect and then, in parentheses, in its objective aspect.

type of personality. Our first approximation to an Erikson typology, therefore, consists of the sixteen logically possible types
listed in Column 5 of Table 11. Columns 2 through 4 list their
counterparts in other typologies, that of Harvey, Hunt and
Schroder having been derived as Erikson's was. The rationale for
these matches will become apparent as Erikson's stages are described in the next few pages.[69]

Table 11 is intended to demonstrate 1) that there is general
correspondence between the four typologies of personality as to
the sequence of developmental stages, and 2) that the developmental sequence follows in a general way the social class hierarchy.
There may be legitimate differences of opinion about the matching
of particular items, but the broad outline of correspondence between the four typologies and between social class and the personality patterning based on developmental limitations seems undeni-
able.

Stage I: Trust and Mistrust

The child's "growth crisis" or major problem in the first stage
is to learn to trust the physical world, people and himself without
losing the elemental sense of caution. He will strike a good balance
between trust and mistrust, one which gives more weight to trust,
if he is cared for in a consistent, comforting, and encouraging way.
This type of upbringing will maximize the child's learning of
cognitive skills not only by exposing him to the necessary materials but also by associating them with pleasurable affect. One
personality based on the positive aspect of this stage would be the
kind that trusts himself and the world enough to "let himself go"
in impulsive, immediately gratifying activity. (The designation of
personality types in each stage and their social class placement are
extrapolations from Erikson's work.) Another is the comfortable
conformist, security-loving and basically optimistic. The social
class value-dimensions which match these two types are found in

TABLE 11
Correspondences Between Personality Types and Their Social Class Placement

Social Class[1]	Adorno's Authoritarian Types	Riesman's Mode-of-Conformity Types	Harvey, Hunt, and Schroder's Stage-Specific Types[2]	Erikson's Stage-Specific Types[2]
LC	High	(Anomic)	(Pre-Stage I)	I+ Trust
WC	High	Tradition-directed		
LC	High	(Anomic)		I– Mistrust
WC	High	Tradition-directed	Stage I: Unilateral Dependence	II+ Autonomy
OMC	High	Inner-directed		
LC	High	Tradition-directed	Transition I	II– Shame and Doubt
WC	High	Tradition-directed		
OMC	High	Inner-directed		
WC	High	Tradition-directed	Stage II: Negative Independence	III+ Initiative
OMC	High	Inner-directed		
NMC	High[3]	Inner-directed		
WC	High	Tradition-directed	Transition II	III– Guilt
OMC	High[3]	Inner-directed		
NMC	High[3]	Inner-directed		
WC	Middle	Tradition-directed	Stage III: Conditional Dependence on Mutuality	IV+ Industry
OMC	Middle	Inner-directed		
NMC	Middle	Other-directed		

Class	Level	Character type	Stage/Transition	Stage label
WC	Middle	Tradition-directed	Transition III	IV– inferiority
OMC	Middle	Inner-directed		
NMC	Middle	Other-directed		
WC	Middle	Tradition-directed		V+ Identity
OMC	Middle	Inner-directed		
NMC	Middle	Other-directed		
WC	Middle	Tradition-directed		V– Identity Diffusion
OMC	Middle	Inner-directed		
NMC	Middle	Other-directed		
NMC	Low	Autonomous Man	Stage IV: Inter-dependence	VI+ Intimacy
OMC	Middle	Inner-directed		VI– Isolation
OMC	Low	Inner-directed		VII+ Generativity
NMC	Low	Autonomous Man		
OMC	Middle	Inner-directed		VII– Self-Absorption
NMC	Low	Autonomous Man		
OMC	Low	Inner-directed		VIII+ Integrity
NMC	Low	Autonomous Man		
OMC	Low	Inner-directed		VIII– Despair
NMC	Low	Autonomous Man		

[1] The abbreviations in this column refer to lower, working, old middle, and new middle class.
[2] The pluses and minuses indicate types organized around the positive or negative aspects of a particular stage.
[3] This is the so-called authoritarianism of the left.

the value systems of the lower and working classes respectively. The personality types of Stage I which give mistrust more weight than trust would be likely to block at both hedonistic action and routinized action and so retreat into sulky cynicism or apathy.

N.B. Personality types which are organized around the positive aspect of a stage can be called "progressive," since they would seem to be more open to further development than types which emphasize the negative aspect. The latter can be called "arrestive" types. In working out a typology based on Erikson's stages, it has been assumed that arrest is possible even in a progressive phase. Thus in Stage I the impulsive hedonist and the conformist are, so to speak, arrested progressive personality types, and the cynic and anomic are arrested arrestives. This breakdown of the typology into progressive and arrestive types and their labelling on the basis of their outstanding characteristic is presented in Table 12.

Stage II: Autonomy and Doubt

In this stage the child's personality is dominated by his newly acquired motoric and mental skills. The child has a great drive to do things for himself. If the parents are patient with him during his struggle for control of himself and of his environment, if they emphasize his successes rather than his failures, he will acquire a sense of mastery and personal potential. If, on the other hand, they are too controlling or too impatient to let the child try out his new powers, he will either rebel against their restrictions or come to doubt his own ability to cope. This is a stage of extremes, and its personality types reflect this: at the progressive pole it produces the compulsive independent and at the arrestive pole the defiant rebel, the defeatist, and the ritualist or compulsive conformist. The various upbringings implicated are in the first and last types those of both the working class and the old middle class, and in the others the same with the addition of the lower class.

Stage III: Initiative and Guilt

If the self-doubt of the previous stage is not overwhelming, the child will now enter a period in which his recently acquired self-control and his new mental and motoric skills are employed in the service of a conscious purpose. He begins to judge his own activities and performances in terms of this purpose and to try out new ones on the same basis. Experimental role-taking is one of the characteristics of this stage, a practice which enables the child to "get hold of" other people and at the same time of himself. Even those children who never develop their role-taking ability to the point of achieving empathy with others do become able at this stage to cooperate and collaborate. Because the individual's standards are now becoming internalized, failure at any of these purposeful tasks produces feelings of guilt. To facilitate the child's development the parents must give him freedom to try out his ideas and provide whatever help and encouragement are needed for him to do so. The personality types that may be extrapolated from the description of successful development are the willing apprentice, the purposeful explorer, and the play-actor. The arrestive types are the timid evader, the overcompensating daredevil, and the self-righteous moralizer. Both working class and middle class orientations seem to be involved in these. When the moralizers are inner-directed, they may become revolutionaries, a middle class action-orientation.

Stage IV: Industry and Inferiority

This stage is marked by an increase of interest in mental ac-

tivities. The ability to reason deductively is developed, and the
usefulness of rules and principles is recognized. The child wants to
know not merely how things work but why they work as they do.
He wants to learn not only to use things but also to make them. If he
is allowed to accomplish these tasks at home and in school, he
experiences a feeling of achievement and power. If he is not
allowed to, he feels incompetent and so inferior to others. The
progressive personality type of this stage is the person with know-
how, whether as a craftsman or as an expert. The arrestive type is
the bungler or under-achiever. The emphasis on activity, rationality, and achievement suggests the middle class value-dimensions,
while the emphasis on the concrete aspects of the environment
suggests those of skilled, creative workers.

Stage V: Identity and Identity Confusion

The problem of this stage is to pull together the skills learned
earlier and put them together into a coherent whole. The young
person's horizon has now expanded so that he can empathize with
other kinds of people, even those of distant places and other
cultures. This broadening of geographical and historical perspectives is accompanied by a deepened understanding of people. New
insights promote compassion, and the ability to grasp abstract
principles leads the adolescent to formulate ideal models against
which individuals, groups, and institutions are judged. This enlarging of the social world may swamp his emerging identity or it
may enable him to perceive his special place and so find himself.
Acquiring an occupational identity is a more concrete approach to
the problem of pulling oneself together.

Parental practices are less important at this stage than in earlier
ones. The peer group, whose influence has been increasing stead-
ily, plus a few adults outside the family virtually replace the

parents as arbiters of taste and behavior. The particularism and primary group orientation nurtured in the peer group of the latency years continue on in the peer group of adolescence. In the typical experience of lower and working class teenagers they are essential dimensions of the enveloping social class value system, thus giving the adolescence of these young people a high degree of continuity with latency and adulthood. Under these conditions rationalism is played down and drowned out by the common sense of the group.

The rationalistic approach to the physical world and to the organizations and institutions of society gives less immediate satisfaction than the traditional, common sense approach. And when rationalism is applied to human relationships and to the development of the self, it is no longer merely irrelevant and boring but actively threatening. If members of a peer group were to make universalistic judgments of one another or to freely express individuality, the solidarity of the peer group would be directly attacked. And if they were forced to judge members of out-groups on the same basis as members of the in-group, the identity of each would be challenged and possibly changed, undermining their security. The whole rationalistic orientation must be suppressed if the blue-collar peer group is to survive and the members to remain comfortably embedded within it.

As middle class adolescents mature, they may move in either direction. If they choose to approach life rationalistically, they move away from peer-group domination and toward inner-direction and even autonomy, though they may never fully achieve either. If the peer group remains the major influence in their lives, they may stall at the adolescent level of in-group conformity or they may attempt to convert the peer group values into broader "humanistic" values and then integrate them with rationalism in a sophisticated form of other-direction. The various resolutions of the adolescent dilemma are summarized in Figure 3.

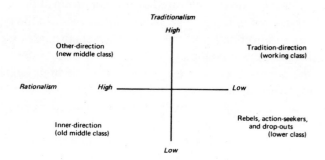

Figure 3. Possible Adolescent Resolutions of
the Traditionalism-Rationalism Dilemma

In terms of personality types, if the adolescent comes from a tradition-directed working class or other-directed new middle class background, he may become a peer-group-oriented faithful follower. If he comes from the inner-directed old middle class, he may become the opposite, a rugged individualist or eccentric. The idealistic type and the faddist could probably be produced by either middle class.

Stage VI: Intimacy and Isolation

In young adulthood Erikson finds the maturing individual struggling with the problem of fully committing himself to others in intimate relationships, whether sexual or non-sexual, without losing his newly won identity in the process. He learns that his self can be complete only when it is shared, but that it can never be shared completely with any one person. As in the case of identity formation, the individual's success or failure at intimacy depends only indirectly and in a general way upon his upbringing. Social conditions and non-familial relationships are now more important as facilitating or diversionary factors. It would seem to be the new middle class subculture which is most likely to facilitate intimacy and produce the progressive personality type of this stage, the sharer. The arrestive type, the loner, looks like an old middle class type.

Stage VII: Generativity and Self-Absorption

In middle age the individual moves beyond a concern for his immediate family and friends to a concern for future generations and the society in which they will live. Self-absorption, the concern for one's own needs and comforts, is perhaps a necessary counterbalance when it is used in a regenerative or restorative way. When it becomes the dominant concern, the individual may be described as an egotist, a type which could most easily occur in the old inner-directed middle class. It could also occur in the new middle class if other-direction were used for self-aggrandizement. When self is subordinated to generativity, the personality type may be called the altruist and seems most likely to occur in the new middle class.

Stage VIII: Integrity and Despair

In old age individuality meets its hardest test, that of dealing gracefully and wisely with the problems of diminishing powers and the inevitability of death. Integrity here involves accepting one's past failures and successes as part of a meaningful life and seeing one's life as flowing into the mainstream of humanity. A philosophical detachment can be developed which keeps existential disgust and despair at bay. Both the old and the new middle classes are capable of developing a sustaining philosophy, though that of the former may be more rigid and self-centered and therefore less mature. Working class people, by contrast, tend to rely on ready-made philosophies provided by the religious or the ethnic subculture.

The existential dilemma is probably felt more strongly by the new middle class than by any other. In attempting to fuse the rational with the traditional value system, this group must reconcile a number of seeming contradictions or opposites. This can be done by enlarging the entire frame of reference enough to admit these as aspects of a greater whole. In the early stage of this synthesis, however, many members of the new middle class will be disappointed and disillusioned when they realize that they must die without seeing much progress in the desired direction. For these people man's humanity is as great a burden as his inhumanity. The old middle class personality types are capable of a tough-minded, rational self-acceptance out of which can evolve a calm acceptance of death: "I've done all that I could, and if that's not good enough, too bad!" For the new middle class, however, this rather self-righteous solace is denied. Instead they must try to surmount existential doubts and disappointments by shaping a philosophy based on the hope that their ideals will be implemented in future generations.

Table 12 summarizes the material of the last few pages: Erikson's stages, their ideal-typical personalities and logical class placement. It should be remembered that Erikson was primarily interested in describing progressive rather than arrestive factors and their behavioral outcomes in the developing child. This has forced us to exaggerate and extrapolate in order to portray adult personalities whose development has been constricted at a particular stage. The labels given to personality types in the descriptions of the eight stages and in Table 12 must be read with this in mind. In the Table they are classified as "progressive" and "arrestive" to indicate their relative openness to further development, the progressives being those which are easier to outgrow and the arrestives those more likely to be developmental dead-ends.

For example, a person suffers an arrest in development in the negative phase of Stage I if he fails to develop a trustful dependency·on others. He may react passively by becoming apathetic and anomic or actively by becoming a disillusioned cynic. Neither reaction encourages change or growth, and so both types are classified as arrestive. A person whose development stalls in the positive phase of Stage I has acquired a basic trust in other people. He may happily and spontaneously act out his impulses or he may settle comfortably into a routine conforming to the habits of those he depends upon. Both reactions permit further progress. In the former case there is at least the possibility that the person will come to pattern his actions in conformity to the norms of some group, if only those of a street gang. Once converted into a routine-seeker or conformist, he may eventually gain enough self-confidence from the approval of his reference group to try things on his own, i.e., progress into Stage II. But progression through the series of progressive personality types established by a social class subculture is not inevitable; permanent arrest or constriction at any progressive personality type is also possible.

Erikson gives two kinds of reasons for developmental arrest: child-rearing techniques which are inappropriate to the child's stage-specific needs and lack of cultural support for development. Harvey, Hunt and Schroder limit themselves to the first kind but specify two types: a lack of openness in child-rearing, which they feel leads to developmental arrest within a stage, and demands for behavior beyond the child's ability to perform, which leads to arrest in a transitional phase.[70] The impingement of cultural influences upon the family is barely acknowledged by these cognitive theorists, and Erikson himself does not deal with them in any detail. A particularly important example is the social class patterning of child-rearing techniques. We have also tried to show that the value system implicit in the non-familial interaction patterns of a social class milieu helps to determine developmental progress or arrest. The social class patterning of these pressures is such that the

TABLE 12
Personality Types (After Erikson) and Their Social Class Placement

Erikson's Developmental Stages[1]	Progressive[2] Personality Types	Arrestive[2] Personality Types	Social Class Placement[3]
I. Mistrust		Apathetic Anomic	LC
		Disillusioned Cynic	LC
Trust	Impulsive Action-Seeker[4]		LC
	Routine-Seeker or Conformist[4]		(LC)[5] WC
II. Shame and Doubt		Paranoid Defeatist	LC WC[6]
		Defiant Rebel	LC WC[6] OMC[6]
		Ritualist or Compulsive Conformist	WC OMC
Autonomy	Compulsive Independent		WC OMC
III. Guilt		Evader	WC OMC NMC
		Daredevil	OMC NMC
		Moralizer	WC OMC NMC
		Revolutionary	OMC NMC[6]
Initiative	Apprentice		WC OMC NMC
	Purposeful Explorer		OMC NMC
	Playactor		NMC

Stage	Type	WC	OMC	NMC
IV. Inferiority	Bungler or Underachiever	WC[6]	OMC[6]	NMC[6]
Industry	Craftsman	WC	OMC	NMC
	Experimenter and Expert		OMC	NMC
V. Identity Confusion	Faddist or Fanatic	WC	OMC	NMC
Identity	Faithful Follower	WC[7]		NMC
	Idealist		OMC	NMC
	Rugged Individualist or Eccentric		OMC	
VI. Isolation	Loner	WC	OMC	
Intimacy	Faithful Sharer			NMC
VII. Self-Absorption	Egotist		OMC	NMC
Generativity	Altruist		(OMC)[7]	NMC
VIII. Despair	Existentialist		(OMC)[7]	NMC
Integrity	Philosopher		(OMC)[7]	NMC

[1] In order of their developmental potential.
[2] "Progressive" and "arrestive" refer to the types' relative openness to further development.
[3] The abbreviations stand for lower class, working class, old middle class, and new middle class.
[4] Gans' terminology, op. cit.
[5] Mothers usually.
[6] Probably this type is downwardly mobile out of this class.
[7] A less mature version of the type.

modal developmental levels in the various social classes correlate with the social class hierarchy.

In Table 12 we have taken the liberty of placing the negative phase of each stage before the positive, although Erikson feels that they are dealt with simultaneously. His reason for placing the positive before the negative lies in his focus upon successful development, a process which depends upon the individual's 1) weighting the positive aspect of a stage more heavily than the negative, and 2) passing through the entire series of stages during his lifetime. We, on the other hand, are interested in what happens when the individual fails to accomplish these tasks. We are also interested in arranging the extrapolated personality types in order of their maturity. Since the individual who weights the negative aspect of a stage more heavily than the positive is making a less progressive and thus less mature choice, it seems logical to place the arrestive types before the progressive types found in a particular stage.

The personality types have been worked out on the basis of presumed behavioral reactions to the values and child-rearing patterns found in specific social classes. The fourth column of Table 12 lists the social class or classes in which each personality type may be expected to appear. The array of this material shows at a glance the tendency for each successive social class level to include more highly developed personality types, in support of our theory. It also shows increasing overlap in personality types with each successive social class level. Presumably the greater the overlap the better the chances of effective communication. There is little or no overlap between the lower class and the working class, once downward mobility is taken into account. Lower class routine-seekers are most likely to be women who aspire to a better life for their children.[71] Perhaps this gap between lower class personality types and those in other levels of society is part of the explanation why lower class people are the perennial outsiders whose behavior is almost impossible for other classes to understand. There is a good deal of overlap between the working class and the old middle class, and predictably more between the old middle class and the new middle class which is emerging from it. Between the working class and the new middle class there is less overlap, calling to mind the confrontation between tradition-directed "hardhats" and other-directed "bleeding hearts."

The overlapping of the social class *ranges* of types is accompanied by extensive class overlapping *within* types. This fact added to the proliferation of types (Table 12 contains almost double the number shown in Table 11) challenges the usefulness of the concept of social class modal personality. Without losing sight of this problem, let us carry forward the search for modal types to its logical conclusion.

Each social class range of personality types can be visualized as distributed along a curve of some sort, but without empirical investigations there is no way of knowing to what extent the curve approaches normality. Though the shape of the curves does not appear in Table 12, two theoretical premises may be useful in locating a centralizing tendency within each social class range. One is the developmental sequence of personality types set forth by Riesman, the other the social class value-dimensions worked out in Chapter 1.

Riesman's work suggests that the central tendency in Western history has been toward progressive types, inasmuch as each of his three major types developed out of its immediate predecessor. Since each successive type occupies a successively higher position in the stratification system from working class through new middle class, it may be inferred that the modal personality types of these classes are progressive rather than arrestive. Having narrowed the field this much, we can narrow it still further by matching each social class value system with the stage of development it best represents.

The lower class is the most difficult case, for Riesman gives no guidance here. Its value-dimensions are most congruent with the developmental characteristics of Stage I, but which if any of the three lower class personality types found there (Table 12) is the modal one is impossible to say. The distribution of types at the bottom of the stratification system may be more rectangular than normal.[72] The working class emphasis on tradition and security and its preference for motoric rather than abstract activities suggest that here development typically peaks in Stage III. Only one progressive type is listed for the working class in this stage (Table 12), the Apprentice. This, then, is the most likely candidate for the working class modal personality, a type characterized by an interest in learning from others and with others how things work and how they are used. The values of the old middle class center around activity, control, and rationality, which are suggestive of Stage IV's more subtle skills, those of the Craftsman and Experimenter-Expert. Since the Experimenter-Expert is the specialty of the old middle class, it is the logical nomination for their modal personality type.

The new middle class's attempted synthesis of the two older sets of values would appear to place it typically in Stage V, the stage of identity crisis. Identity may be achieved either by following people or by following abstract ideals. Although the typical member of the new middle class is greatly interested in ideals, he probably prefers to have them embodied in people rather than floating about in words and dreams. This can be inferred from his fusing of individualism with primary group orientation. As an Idealist he would be condemned to a good deal of loneliness, but as a Faithful Follower he can work at implementing his ideals in company with a group of like-minded people. The new middle class modal personality is probably one that can best handle the problems of identity within a group of this kind.

For whatever they are worth, then, our nominations for social class modal types are the Apprentice for the working class, the Experimenter-Expert for the old middle class, and the Faithful

Follower for the new middle class. No central tendency can be detected in the lower class, though their stage of arrest (Stage I) emerges more clearly than that of any other class. Their isolated position is underlined by the gap which separates their characteristic level of development from that of the working class (Stage III) and their entrapment by the preponderance of arrestive types.

In view of the considerable social class overlapping both within and between developmental stages, it is probably more heuristic and undoubtedly more accurate to compare social classes in terms of their ranges than in terms of specific modal personality types. As mentioned earlier, even by this measure the social class differentials are readily apparent. Perhaps in the future a more discriminating means of identifying the central tendency within each range will suggest itself.

CONCLUSION

Four ways of examining and classifying personality have been described. All are based upon the notion of a developmental continuum which progresses from stimulus-bondage to domination of the stimulus and represents the ideal-typical life cycle. All are in agreement that interruptions of this progression serious enough to bring about arrests in development thereby produce variations in adult personality. Therefore all of them allow for the working out of a set of personality types based upon the consequences of arrest at various developmental levels.

Each of the four approaches personality differently. Harvey, Hunt and Schroder's cognitive typology emphasizes the role played by the intellective processes in determining the degree of power the individual can exercise over his world. Adorno's affective typology focuses upon variations in the emotional experiences of children and how these produce differential expectations of control over the self and others, ranging from defensive authoritarianism to a confident and tolerant independence. Riesman bases his typology upon historical variations in the mode of conformity or source of authority instilled into people by their society and their social class. The personality types that result range from the tradition-directed to the autonomous. The broadest analysis of development is Erikson's. He too describes a succession of stages leading from initial dependence upon the world to eventual physical and intellectual mastery of it. The stage-specific personality types are set down in Table 11 in matching sequence with those of the other typologies. And since Table 11 also indicates the presumed social class location of the various types, it serves as a summary of the chapter to that point. It shows a general correspondence between the four personality typologies and a tendency for social class level to be positively correlated with developmental level. To make a still broader summary, it may now be observed that the conclusions of the personality theorists corroborate the conclusions drawn from the more specialized materials of Chapters 2, 3, and 4, both in terms of the developmental process and in terms of the effects of social class membership upon it.

Since Erikson's explication of development is the most comprehensive one, it is more reasonable to search for social class modal personalities here than in the more limited typologies. Table 12 shows that when the implications of his formulation of each stage are extrapolated, almost twice as many personality types emerge as are shown in Table 11, where only stage-specific types are projected. This makes the search for modal personalities more difficult and more questionable, for although the social class correlation with developmental level is much clearer in Table 12 than in Table 11, the extensive overlapping of social classes within and between developmental stages casts a shadow over the utility of the modal personality concept. Some hints as to central tendencies appear in the necessity to nominate progressive types shown by Riesman and in the class value systems, which suggest the following designations:

Social Class	Stage of Arrest	Modal Personality
Lower Class	Stage I	?
Working Class	Stage III	Apprentice
Old Middle Class	Stage IV	Experimenter-Expert
New Middle Class	Stage V	Faithful Follower

At this moment, however, a more heuristic basis of comparison is the social class range of types, a comparison which though less pointed still illuminates the developmental differentials between classes.

6

Implications and Applications

Where does all of this take us? Any knowledge is desirable in and of itself, but its value increases in proportion to its utility. This may be in the realm of theory, of practicality, or—best of all—a combination of both. Two of the developmental sequences just described, Riesman's and Erikson's, suggest that the relationship between social class and personality development should be set into a broad historical framework. When this is done, a social-psychological theory of history emerges which explains the derivation of the social class/developmental relationship, predicts the direction in which it will move, and implies certain consequences for the structure of society. Knowing the probable direction of change and the processes by which it takes place makes it possible to intervene, supporting beneficial trends and dismantling harmful ones.

A SOCIAL-PSYCHOLOGICAL THEORY OF HISTORY

Riesman's formulation is in the mainstream of sociological thought about the direction of Western history. Toennies[1] in fact based sociology upon the study of history, which he perceived as moving from a *Gemeinschaft* or communal type of social organization to a *Gesellschaft* or formal type. That is, it was moving away from an affectively based, naive conformity (which Riesman calls tradition-direction) toward a cognitively based, individualistic, contractual form of association (which Riesman calls inner-direction). Durkheim[2] similarly contrasted two types of societies: those held together mechanically by the unquestioning acceptance of cultural tradition and those held together organically by recognition of mutual dependence and by rational calculation. Further he suggested that change from one type to the other occurred as population increases inevitably brought about greater division of labor and so greater complexity. Riesman, too, sees population growth as the prime mover in changing modes of conformity and in producing corresponding changes in social character.[3] But it is probably Max Weber's work which has had the most immediate effect upon Riesman's thinking.

Weber developed the concepts of traditionalism and rationalism and called the transforming process of moving from one toward the other rationalization. He examined the process of rationalization most thoroughly in the areas of religion, political control[4] and economics,[5] and showed evidence of its operation in the arts as well.[6] In analyzing the development of rationalistic attitudes toward economics, he pointed to Protestant individualism, "this inner isolation of the individual,"[7] as one of the antecedents, and it is this aspect of his thought which seems to have strongly influenced Riesman in his formulation of the inner-directed personality type.[8]

The idea that the trend from traditionalism to rationalism in Western history represents increasing maturity or a rising developmental level was set forth at the end of the nineteenth century by Toennies, when he compared the mentality characteristic of *Gemeinschaft* society to that of a woman, a youth, an uneducated person. It is, he said, a mentality dominated by sentiment, while the evolving *Gesellschaft* mentality, typified by that of a man, an elder, or an educated person, is dominated by conscious calculation.[9] And so the proposition that the rationalistic value system of the middle class represents a higher level of development than the traditionalistic value system of the blue-collar classes can claim a respectable ancestry. Riesman follows Toennies in this but goes a step further to suggest an emerging neo-humanistic value system, that of other-directed man. It is tempting to interpret his sequence as a Hegelian progression from thesis (present-oriented traditionalism) to antithesis (future-oriented rationalism) to synthesis (neo-humanism). Figure 4 shows how Riesman matches sociocultural development with personality development. Whether one's starting point is social theory, social class, or sociocultural development, the course of Western history ultimately appears to be characterized not only by technological progress but by psychological progress as well, *pace* the current "dehumanization" school of thought.

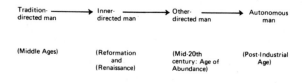

Figure 4. Riesman's Hypothesis

Erikson has examined personality from the point of view of the individual rather than that of history. Nevertheless, in deriving specific forms of social structure from successive developmental levels of the life cycle, he suggests a rationale for sociocultural development as well. In Table 13 Erikson's stages of personality development are listed along with their related social structures. The extreme right-hand column indicates the institutional forms which embody these structures. The order in which they appear

TABLE 13

Individual Development and the Institutional Development of Society[1]

Life Stage (in modern society)	Growth Crisis	Related Social Structure	Institutional Form
I. Infancy	Trust and Mistrust	Organized faith	Nuclear family Religion
II. Play Age	Autonomy and Shame-Doubt	Law and order	Kinship Polity
III. Play Age	Initiative and Guilt	Moral law	Age-grading and Clubs; Justice
IV. School Age	Industry and Inferiority	Technology	Guilds Economy
V. Adolescence	Identity and Identity Diffusion	Ideology	Epic Poetry and Drama Communication
VI. Young Adulthood	Intimacy and Isolation	Organized co-operation and competition	Recreation Philanthropy
VII. Adulthood	Generativity (or Authority) and Self-Absorption	Education and tradition	Education Science
VIII. Senescence	Integrity and Despair	Literature and philosophy	(The Fine Arts)[2] Philosophy

[1] After Erikson and Jones. Richard M. Jones, *Fantasy and Feeling in Education* (New York: New York University Press, 1968), pp. 130-1. The point that Column 3 suggests the sequence of sociocultural evolution is made on p. 220.

[2] The fine arts tend to resist structuring, but if they were to form a separate institution, it would probably be the last to differentiate out.

represents the order in which they would presumably emerge as separate institutions in the ideal-typical development of society, although the point of emergence is not necessarily the point of their highest development.

Anthropologists feel that the family and religion were probably the first institutions of human society and were relatively unspecialized. That is, they performed a wide variety of functions, many of which require separate, specialized institutions in a complex society. The family and religion were embedded in a network of kindred which might comprise a clan, moiety, or the entire tribe. Political organization has been at various times a function of the kinship network and a function of religion. In more evolved societies it has freed itself from these entanglements to become a separate institution, partly in response to the pressures of population growth. Similarly economic activities, which were traditionally carried on as an integral part of family life, have gradually removed elsewhere (e.g., into guilds) and have developed new norms, roles and statuses as well as new relationships with other institutions. This process of increasing specialization, separation, and autonomy is called differentiation.

Let us examine the possibility that there is a fixed order of institutional differentiation to match the fixed order of individual development and see how far it can be sustained. A separate, specialized polity can hardly develop without the family and kinship network to provide the personnel, the basic social integration, and the substructure of ascribed statuses through which authority can be channeled. Age-grades and clubs, which cut across kinship lines to provide a more formal basis for group solidarity and specialized functions, cannot very well be established without the stability provided by the kinship and/or political organization. Justice administered earlier by other institutions can now begin to differentiate itself from them, though it still derives its authority from religion or the polity. A separate economy rests in turn upon the bases of stability, specialization, and extra-familial association, as well as on the impartial administration of justice.

From this point on, the line of development ceases to be directly epigenetic, except in traditional societies with a wealthy enough economy to support the early emergence of epic poetry and drama as a separate institution. Since they do not appear to be logically dependent each upon the previous one, the institutions of communication, recreation, philanthropy, education, and science may differentiate out simultaneously rather than sequentially. The factor which makes such explosive development possible is the rationalization of the economy, since this makes available the human and material resources necessary for each of these budding institutions to function in relative independence. The fine arts are included in Table 13 for the sake of completion, but with the reminder that in their highest forms they can never be fully institutionalized since they depend upon personal vision and creativity rather than upon group norms and statuses.

Figure 5 diagrams the suggested sequence of institutional differentiation. Although for the most part the arrows go in one direction, the sequence should be understood as a feedback system, with each subsequent development affecting the form and content of its antecedents.

Societies which have not developed a full set of differentiated institutions can be considered to suffer from arrested development just as individuals do, and in fact *when* individuals do. Probably a given institution cannot become sufficiently differentiated to be identified as a separate entity unless or until enough individuals in the society have reached the appropriate level of development so as to staff it with capable personnel. That is, there must be enough people who can conceive of and interact on the basis of specialized norms, statuses and roles in the area of life organized by the institution. The term ''arrested development'' as applied to societies carries with it the same caveat as it does when applied to personalities: it does not mean that all abilities or functions belong-

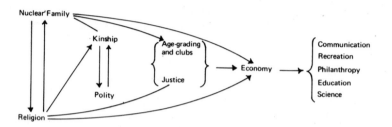

Figure 5. The Sequence of Institutional Differentiation
(after Erikson and Jones)

ing to higher levels are completely unattainable forevermore. Rather it means that society, like the individual, undergoes a sort of premature closure which discourages further differentiation and change, thereby stunting most areas of development beyond that point.

The more concrete the general level of mental operations in a society, the stronger its tendency toward closure, toward relying on available solutions and instant meaning, toward resisting change and living by habit and tradition. In the case of our own society, we have found that concrete operations are characteristic of the personality types most frequently found in the two lower classes. In the context of Western history, Riesman's descriptions of successively emerging personality types indicate that the earlier the type, the more concrete its mental operation. Looking at the whole array of societies, Werner finds that concrete operations are more characteristic of people living in primitive than in advanced societies,[10] and Church explains why in terms which link the level of individual development with that of sociocultural development. His explanation makes the same developmental comparison between societies that we have made between social classes. Intrinsic to both is the notion of developmental arrest. Church points out that

> we are all born into the sphere of primitive experience, with very similar (although by no means identical) capacities for learning, and . . . our cultural experience develops our capacities in various ways. The more primitive culture institutionalizes, stabilizes, and elaborates our earlier forms of experience, whereas the more advanced culture tends to transform them and replace them with new forms.[11]

This position is tellingly documented by three studies of cognitive growth which compare children of traditional cultures with children who have been exposed to modern, urban culture.[12] In each case the former are found not only to develop their cognitive abilities more slowly but also to stop far short of the developmental level of the latter group. Bruner summarizes the results in these words:

> If the child lives in an advanced society such as our own, he becomes ''operational'' (to use the Genevan term for thinking symbolically), and by age five, six, or seven, given cultural supports, he is able to apply the fundamental rules of category, hierarchy, function, and so forth, to the world as well as to his words. . . . if he is growing up in a native village of Senegal, among native Eskimos, or in a rural *mestizo* village in Mexico [however] he may not achieve this ''capacity.'' Instead, he may remain at a level of manipulation of the environment that is concretely ikonic and strikingly lacking in symbolic structures—though his language may be [intricate and richly elaborated] in these regards.[13]

It is probably necessary at this point to state flatly that the adult member of a primitive or traditional society cannot be equated with the child member of a modern one, even though this should be clear from the earlier discussion of arrested development. This point is a major theme in Werner's early work on development.[14] It comes up again in Greenfield's work when she argues against the old assumption that primitive adults have less of something common to all other people[15] and therefore represent the childhood of mankind. In point of fact primitive adults do have less of something, though it is not something common to *all* other people: they have less experience and training in what Bruner calls "the symbolic representation of experience."[16] This lack compels them to operate on a lower level of cognitive development than people in more advanced cultures, and it was the observed similarity between their level of mental operation and that of children in advanced cultures[17] which led to the objectionable equation in the first place. Once a careful distinction is made between the *observed* level of operation among primitive people and their *potential* level of operation, given a more highly developed cultural experience, the difficulty evaporates. The same distinction must be made in discussing social class differences in developmental level, that they are sociocultural in origin and tell the observer nothing about the *potential* of either individuals or groups.

All of these contributions combine to produce the theory that types of societies can be placed on a continuum which represents simultaneously a scale of institutional differentiation and a scale of modal personality development. Primitive society is lowest on the scale, as the type characterized by the least amount of differentiation and the highest proportion of concrete mental operations, followed by the feudal, industrial, and post-industrial types. If this progressive trend in Western history is projected into the future, it predicts an increasingly differentiated society and a shift toward more highly developed personality types. The confidence level of this prediction is higher than most because it is based not only on inertial momentum from the past but also on the direction inherent in human development. Here phylogeny recapitulates ontogeny.

Given confidence in the general prediction, it can be further specified by working out the institutional characteristics of our future society on the basis of the trend in personality development. When most members of a society are in the stage of concrete operations, strong external controls are needed, and these are provided by unspecialized, overlapping institutions. When most people have reached a relatively abstract stage and have achieved a high degree of internal control, far fewer institutional controls will be needed. Pushing this sequence to its theoretical conclusion, it would ultimately produce Riesman's "autonomous man," who can get along with a minimum of structure. Possibly this is akin to what Marx had in mind when he spoke of the withering away of the state. The size of social units is a variable which must enter into the calculation. The larger the population or membership of a social unit, the more need for formal controls in order to facilitate interaction between relative strangers. The state is one outcome of this need. Figure 6 shows the effects of population level and modal personality development within a society upon the characteristics of its institutions. Centralization refers to the increasing size and power of interactional units, while specialization refers to the narrowing of their functions.

The arrows indicate the ideal-typical historical sequence. It starts in the upper right-hand corner with the simplest or most primitive society and continues in the lower right-hand corner with a society complex enough to support a considerable population. The lower left-hand corner represents the stage into which our own society seems to be moving, a stage characterized by a general loosening of institutional controls. Finally the move toward the upper left-hand corner represents the projection of the historico-developmental theory into the future, when decentralization of population as well as of institutions may take place. That is, the population level of groups will be lower, whatever the total popu-

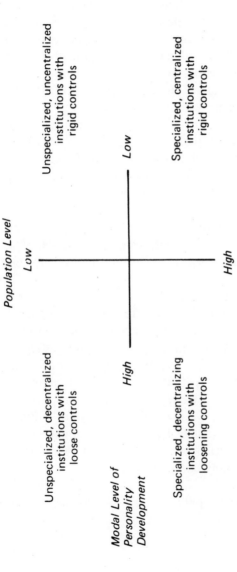

Figure 6. The Institutional Characteristics of Society Relative to Its Population and Modal Developmental Level

lation of society may be, as a result of the decentralization of institutions. Already the trend toward decentralization is visible in many areas, e.g., the handing back of functions by the federal government to state governments; the pressure for local control of schools; the increasing autonomy of corporate divisions; the gradual transfer of mental patients, juvenile delinquents, and homeless children out of large establishments and into foster homes or their equivalent; the diversification of life-styles; the population movement from the city to the suburbs.[18]

Life in a society characterized by smaller groups, less specialized institutions with looser controls, and a high modal level of personality development would be simpler than in ours without sacrificing any of our present variety. Church explains this paradox as it applies to personality development in this way:

> Developmentally, abstraction is not merely a movement from the particular to the general, from the abundance of the concrete to the austerity of the abstract. It also is the unification and simplification of experience, the reduction of complexity to orderly, manageable principles. So much stress has been laid on development as differentiation, as increase in complexity that we must emphasize the complement of differentiation, hierarchic integration, by which differentiated perceptions, knowledge, and processes are brought together in new, higher-order patterns which permit simplicity and directness of action. If we speak of integrity of functioning as a mark of maturity, we mean that the mature individual is simpler than the immature. His simplicity, however, is richly textured and tapestried and expresses the harmonious working together of many components.[19]

This description may apply equally well to the society of the future.

The theoretically based prediction that our future history will be characterized by further progress both on the societal and the personality levels would have to be modified by evidence of trends whose net effects seem likely to be destructive rather than constructive. Looking at the ferment within our society today, it is tempting to say that all of the current trends are destructive. Our institutions are in a state of siege. The credibility, indeed the viability of our government is in question. Minority groups and deviants threaten the social order in the urgency of their demands for opportunity and self-determination. The quality of life poses basic scientific, economic, and social dilemmas. What is there in our present situation that can possibly justify an optimistic prediction?

The historico-developmental theory suggests that the very problems we perceive and the fact of our perceiving them should be considered causes for optimism. As someone said recently, a smokestack belching smoke used to represent prosperity, but today it is seen as a source of pollution. The perception of despoliation and dysfunction either in the physical or in the social environment is an essential preliminary to dismantling old structures of thought and action in these areas and seeking new ways of solving problems. Is it not in fact the most terrifying events of recent times which are having the most profoundly constructive or reconstructive effects upon our society?

—Assassination has made the American people extremely sensitive to the use of violence as a weapon of personal and group dissent, as a means of governmental control, and as a prime ingredient in the mass media's presentation of news and entertainment.
—The Viet Nam war along with its corruption scandals, its deliberate massacres, and its manipulation of facts has led the public into a serious debate about Presidential power, the

    morality of our foreign policy, the credibility of the military and the CIA, the economic effects of war, and the value of human life.

—The civil disorders and strident demands of minority groups such as blacks, prison inmates, women, and homosexuals have led to the legitimization of their grievances and the beginning of redress, not only on the part of official agencies but on the part of the public as well.

—The drug problem among young people has given the mental health movement new impetus and is educating the public about addiction of all kinds. Middle class people, who used to lump this problem with poor housing, low educational level and other social disabilities, are now sadly aware that it can appear at all levels of society. As a result a new tolerance for personal problems of all kinds is emerging.

—The ecological crisis, whose full import is beginning to be grasped by the public, has made people conscious as never before of their dependence upon one another and of their responsibilities to future generations. Certain privileges must be restricted if others are to be enjoyed. This involves the renunciation of many immediate gratifications, and people seem increasingly willing to look toward the future.

All of these problems and crises can be viewed as developmental experiences that are helping the American people to mature. "Sweet are the uses of adversity. . . ."

According to this line of thought, the pessimistic interpretation of current affairs grows out of the temporary dislocations accompanying institutional decentralization and the loosening of controls. These in turn arise from the attempts of institutions to adapt to the new demands upon them, and so the discomfort that individuals suffer in the process is largely unavoidable. It is interesting to note, however, that this discomfort and pessimism can arise from two diametrically opposed complaints about social change.

The new middle class typically complains that it is too slow, and the old middle and working classes that it is too fast.

The position of the new middle class is based on the neo-humanistic value system associated with the other-directed personality type. It produces a heightened empathy with all kinds of people, a sensitive conscience, and a passionate vision of a happier society. Little wonder that neo-humanists are often despondent about present conditions and impatient with those who accept them! Having developed beyond the mainstream of society, they perceive social problems as evidence of cultural lag. Yet the emergence of the neo-humanistic value system is probably the most encouraging single sign of progress in our time. When one remembers that the rationalistic value system has been with us for some 500 years and the traditionalistic one since early antiquity, the extraordinary feat of our era in bringing forth neo-humanism becomes apparent. We are not culturally dead yet. An especially constructive feature of the new value system is the fact that instead of taking off in the opposite direction, as rationalism did, neo-humanism picks up the cultural strands of antiquity and plaits them together with those of the more immediate past. In so doing it promises to reconcile the ideals of the lower echelons of society with those of the upper echelon. Perhaps this is the sense in which Marx's ''classless society'' can be achieved.

A larger group taking umbrage at the adaptive changes in institutions is composed of people not yet developmentally ready for them. Old middle and working class people predominate here, the latter feeling the greater anxiety because of the undermining of the traditional authorities that they revere. The pessimism of these groups is based on both the direction and the rapidity of cultural change. Lower class people may be the only group to find the trend toward decentralization and looser controls initially congenial, for both cynical and exploitative reasons. In the long run, however, as society comes to require more and more of individuals and to do less and less for them, people of the present lower class personality types would find themselves progressively less able to cope. As optimism began to grow in the higher echelons of society, pessimism would deepen at the lowest, if the social class modal levels of personality development were to remain stationary. In the next section we shall see how this may be prevented.

If our society existed in isolation, the optimistic prediction might prove hard to challenge, but such is not the case. Our society is an advanced one, and the more advanced a society the more involved it is in the economic and political affairs of others. Again, if all societies were at somewhere near the same level of development, this would not matter. Unfortunately they are not. Over one hundred of them, comprising over two billion people, have yet to reach the economic "take-off" point,[20] the point at which they can sustain their own industrialization without large infusions of foreign aid or grinding sacrifices at home. Yet the peoples of these economically backward nations know how the rest of the world lives and cannot see why they should wait another fifty to one hundred years to reach the same point. This means that about two thirds of the population of the world, the vast majority of whom are non-Western, are in a politically explosive mood. Whether they and their governments will permit our society or the West generally to continue undisturbed along the historical path of development that theory predicts for it is the critical question of the next century.

If the average level of personality development in our society continues to rise as the Riesman and Erikson materials suggest it has been doing for centuries, it should be reflected in more foresighted foreign policy and aid programs. This is one way in which the problem of non-Western economic development may be met. A more rational and responsible public would elect a more rational and responsible government and support international programs which would be unacceptable today. The growing appreciation of others' needs, limited in past centuries to members of one's own primary, ethnic, and religious groups, is now extending beyond national and cultural boundaries. As consciousness is raised, conscience expands; the history of public attitudes toward the Vietnamese is a recent example. The promise of further increases in the average maturity level is apparent today in the widespread revulsion of the young against materialism and violence, both of which represent the concrete end of the developmental scale. Such attitudes will ease the strain of accepting a lower standard of living, if this is necessary, and the strain of dealing with nations which are in a phase of truculent chauvinism. And a higher level of cognitive skill will give people more understanding of and patience with the problems of the international monetary system, the balance of trade, and other politico-economic issues. The question is whether our society and others in the West can mature rapidly enough to accept a parental responsibility for the developing nations or will continue to treat them as tag-along younger siblings.

GUIDELINES FOR PUBLIC POLICY

If the line of thinking pursued up to this point is accepted, its implications for public policy are clear: the historical trend toward a rising average level of personality development should be supported by every means available. A few scattered programs are already in operation, and a few promising tools are lying about. But before these can be refined, redesigned, or replaced, the behavioral sciences must come together on a broad, theoretically solid footing. The area of human development may provide the best meeting place, since this concept transcends time and culture. The first half of this chapter is an example of how development can serve as a rallying point around which sociology, psychology, history, and anthropology may be effectually deployed.

When agreement on basic principles and practices has been reached, developmental psychology can take the leading role *pro tem*. Its first task might well be to define the degrees of maturity at once more broadly and more specifically. That is, the various areas of development would be carefully identified and the stage-specific indicators of progress and arrest for each separate area worked out. A good beginning has been made; e.g., by Harvey, Hunt, and Schroder[21] in the cognitive area, but further analyses are necessary, and the work of scattered investigators needs to be assembled within a master framework acceptable to behavioral scientists generally. The interrelations between areas must be elucidated, too, so that messy concepts like intelligence and adjustment are either narrowed to a sharp point or else frankly derived from the larger profile of relative maturity.

Since the ultimate objective is to learn how to facilitate development not only in children but also in adults, it will be necessary to translate child norms for a given stage within each area into adult norms. This will be anything but a simple, automatic process, inasmuch as an adult personality whose progress is arrested at a certain stage cannot be directly compared with the personality of a child passing through the same stage because of the adult's experiences subsequent to the arrest. Probably several sets of norms calibrated to other types of measures must be worked out for each check-point. Once these are established, reliable measuring devices based upon them can be developed, and standardized testing becomes possible. At this point developmental psychology can begin to offer detailed practical guidance to program-planners.

Meanwhile, social scientists will have been broadening and deepening their knowledge of structural change in their respective fields in order to discover how to guide and coordinate it. Whether programs of change should start at the top of the system or at the bottom, with structures or with people, is a chicken-or-egg controversy. According to the historico-developmental theory there is a reciprocal relationship between the form and functioning of a social structure and the maturity level of its members. In terms of policy-making and programming, this means that both should be tackled at the same time in a coordinated and interdisciplinary effort.

A fragmented approach to structural reform is one of the characteristics of democratic societies. Rival interest groups pull policy-makers this way and that in the absence of a superordinate goal upon which everyone can agree. Perhaps the behavioral sciences are now in the position to correct this by proposing one acceptable to all because it is framed in terms of people rather than in terms of things or institutions. A national commitment to help all citizens achieve their highest potential development would seem intrinsically more worthwhile than the goal of producing a higher GNP or broadening the democratic base or assuming world leadership. Therefore it should prove to be a more unifying and more highly motivating goal for all. And although the means of implementing it would still be matters of dispute, it would provide an ultimate standard of reference for the disputants.

The reader who doubts this proposition should ask himself the following questions: Will greater national wealth automatically produce a more intelligent and responsible populace, and which achievement would make this a better country to live in? To what extent will our democracy be enhanced by greater participation while a large proportion of the people remain concrete-minded and authoritarian? How desirable is a government's aspiration to world leadership when its domestic leadership is responsible for the cynicism and alienation of large numbers of its people?

In addition to providing a broader basis for national unity, the goal of facilitating human development has the advantage of being in the mainstream of history. According to the historico-developmental theory, trends are already underway which are pressing the average developmental level higher and higher. An obvious move for social planners, then, is to identify those trends which foster development and those that arrest it, and to design programs which strengthen the former and phase out the latter.

Since the current trend toward decentralization has already been identified as one which fosters development (in Figure 6 and the explanation of it) let's use it as an example of possible procedure, though anti-materialism, tolerance, or some other would serve as well. Before the policy of decentralization were applied to a given agency or institution, a developmental survey of the population to be affected by it would be carried out, using the tests devised by developmental psychology. This would provide information on the basis of which the planners could gear the methods and pace of their program to the characteristics and needs of the clientele. Later, when the program was underway, periodic retesting of the clientele could be carried out to measure the effectiveness of the program and to suggest possible modifications. Comparing it with other programs of decentralization in other agencies and institutions would provide additional means for judging its effectiveness. Such comparative information could also be used to produce an index of the progress of the trend which could serve as one of a set of social indicators monitoring the vital signs of society.[22] The social indicators would be read in terms of the national developmental goal and would point to areas needing special attention. Used in this way they would provide for a more equitable approach to social problems and a more balanced national growth. It is easy to see that broad advances in the social sciences are needed to accomplish any such high-level planning and coordination successfully.[23]

In sum, the historico-developmental theory offers a new type of national goal based on the needs of the 'whole man' rather than on his economic, political, physical, or other segmental needs. Policies resting on this base should produce a unifying as well as a unified approach to structural reform. Programs to implement them will have to be designed to fit all stages of the life cycle and of development. At every point the need is clear for more detailed developmental norms, reliable tests, greater social science expertise, and continuous research into all phases of human development, if behavioral scientists are to provide valid counsel for public policy-makers and program administrators.

At the present time more is known about changing individuals than about changing social structures. Most of the individualized programs which foster personality development are found in the school system, because childhood is the best time for this, and also because children are conveniently accessible in school. Whether found in school or out, here or abroad, the programs about to be described demonstrate that certain means of raising the maturity level in individuals and small groups are available to us right now.

Since the early years of life are crucially important for the child's later development,[24] this is the period in which it is logical to invest the greatest amount of time and energy. The fact that the learning of cognitive skills in infants and pre-schoolers could be greatly facilitated by personal attention and mental stimulation was brought out in Chapter 2 in the reports of experimental work with the retarded and comparative observations of maternal behavior. The answer to inadequate attention and stimulation is some sort of training for mothers and/or placing the child in a better environment, such as a day care center. A few experimental programs have been set up to show how mothers can be helped to improve their child-rearing style, but our society has made no structural provisions for teaching young people to be adequate parents. The public schools may offer a smattering of information, but for most people their main source of information is the mass media. Women's magazines and specialized books reach a large number but only of those oriented toward reading. Television, which reaches the largest number of all, does not attempt to cover child-rearing and development on a regular basis. Thus an enormous opportunity to cultivate children's personalities through the education of parents and future parents has been ignored.

Instead, official agencies have concentrated on programs that bypass parents, such as setting up day care centers and making kindergarten compulsory. The whole trend is toward removing the child from home at an earlier age and keeping him away from home longer in order that the school can provide more of the services that used to be provided by the family—recreation, guidance, health care, feeding, and sex education are some examples. Official policy and practice in this area are supported by at least two long-run factors—economic pressures on the family which have increasingly pushed mothers into the job market, and the emancipation of women, currently appearing as the women's liberation movement.

One significant indicator of this trend is the recent surge of interest in communal child-rearing among the style-setting stratum of the new parental generation, upper middle class young people in their twenties. There are probably a number of reasons for it, including their interest in liberal and radical solutions for social problems, the personal problem of being tied down during the search for identity and the other-directed preference for group activities and group decisions. Whatever the reasons, these young style-setters are creating a climate of opinion which will strengthen the trend toward the schools and other official agencies taking over the socialization of children. In the face of this situation, developing separate programs to educate parents may have to be regarded as a temporary expedient, to be phased out as the jurisdiction of official agencies reaches younger and younger children.

A prototypical day care program oriented toward development is carried on in Little Rock in the same elementary school that the children will later attend.[25] Funded by the Office of Child Development, it is a cooperative venture of the University of Arkansas, the Little Rock school system, and the State Department of Education. Care is provided from 7:00 AM to 5:00 PM in a program that stresses emotional as well as cognitive development. It is reported that:

After one year at the Center, day-care preschoolers registered a gain of 12 IQ points as compared to 2 points for a control group on the outside. On achievement tests involving language and numbers concepts, Center children gained 16 scaled points more than other youngsters. In a test that involved associating spoken words with pictures, day-care four-year-olds outscored a control group in the same age range.[26]

This program is of special interest because of its funding by a federal agency and because it was reported in a nationally distributed magazine section for Sunday newspapers as a suggested model for structural change. "[The Little Rock program] of early, continuous, away-from-home education for youngsters starting almost in infancy is attracting deep interest elsewhere and, if it spreads, could change the face of American education."[27] A visitor from the Child Study Center at Yale is quoted as saying, "I see the . . . program as potentially a model for the schools of the future."[28] Preschool education and day care may introduce developmental psychology into the council chambers of the power elite.

An essential element in cognitive development is the learning of the "formal language" which enables communication to reach a more abstract level than that on which the "public language" operates. It was pointed out in Chapter 2 that middle class parents teach both to their children, but that familiarity with the formal language diminishes at lower social class levels. Developmentally oriented day care like that provided in the Little Rock program would reduce or eliminate deficiencies in linguistic skill. By the time the child reaches school age, it may be too late or too difficult to help him overcome them.

The deliberate teaching of cognitive skills is seen as the major function of the public school system, and so a good deal of experimentation has been carried out in an attempt to improve performance. Most of it has been general, with the objective of discovering what these skills consist of and how they are acquired, but some is aimed at developing better specific training methods and at tailoring teaching methods to children's cognitive styles.[29] An example of a specific training method is "brainstorming," which is useful in developing "intellectual fluency" or the free flow of possible solutions to a problem. Fluency has been found by factor analysis to be one of the three major factors in creative thinking.[30] Another approach to improving cognitive skills is the reorienting of teaching methods to emphasize the principles that underlie study materials and the strategies for finding them, rather than emphasizing their content. An example of this is the inductive "discovery method" which leads students to use concrete facts to build abstract structures of meaning.[31] Developmental psychologists and other behavioral scientists are acting as full partners and often as leaders in the development of new curricula based on such methods.[32]

Role-taking is the use of cognitive imagination to create within oneself the structure and meaning of another's behavior. In recent years the technique of deliberate role-playing in mock situations has been transposed from the laboratory into the classroom. It can be used to produce a variety of outcomes favorable to personality development, such as increased sensitivity to others,[33] thinking in terms of long range consequences,[34] and thinking of more solutions to problems or intellectual fluency.[35] Since these three outcomes would seem logically to conduce toward more abstract mental operations, role-playing appears to be a promising technique for fostering psychological growth.

Passing from the cognitive to the affective side of personality development, we find that developmental psychology affords fewer applications. This is not surprising when it is remembered that the model of personality development is based on cognitive learning. So far as the young child is concerned, the major finding has been that adequate affective experiences are essential to cognitive development, and so it has been necessary to treat the two together. Once the child reaches school age, he spends approximately one third of his waking hours on an annual basis in school, where the emphasis is on the development of cognitive skills. Gestures are made in the direction of "mental health" and "emotional adjustment," but no systematic attempt is made to cultivate the moral and emotional aspects of personality.[36]

Out of his experience as a consultant on a project to design a new social science curriculum for the fifth grade, psychiatrist Richard Jones advocates the "cultivation of emotional issues in classrooms, whether by design or in response to the unpredictable, [as a] means to the ends of instructing the children in the [cognitive] subject matter."[37] To accomplish this properly, he feels, a new theory of instruction is needed: one which would "prescribe not only optimal levels of intellectual uncertainty, risk and relevance but also optimal levels of emotional involvement and personal curiosity."[38] Jones has attempted to provide this by showing how Erikson's stages of development can be used as a teacher's guide in making classroom subject matter relevant to the child's affective as well as his cognitive development. This involves three interrelated steps:

1 coordination of developmental issues with curricular issues;
2 coordination of cognitive skills with emotional and imaginal skills;
3 coordination of classroom management with instruction.[39]

Jones feels strongly that the realistic portrayal of life in other cultures which is provided by film and other materials of the new social science curriculum offers teachers a unique opportunity to enhance affective development and at the same time harness it to cognitive learning.[40] Gallagher goes still farther, suggesting that "If ways could be found to improve personal autonomy and reduce dependence, it may be possible to broaden productive thinking, perhaps even in the absence of specific cognitive exercises or training."[41]

Bronfenbrenner emphasizes the lack of effective moral training in the school system. Noting that "In American schools, training for action consistent with social responsibility and human dignity is at best an extra-curricular activity,"[42] he advocates that they provide children with experiences embodying the dominant values of society as a means of character training. In his observations of nursery school children in Russia he found them raised in peer groups which mirror the values of the adult world rather than specialized values of their own.[43] The learning of cooperation, generosity, and other desired forms of behavior is not left to chance but is emphasized and practiced with the help of the teacher. Discipline is gradually taken over by the peer group itself, as the children grow older. By the time they reach high school, the children are highly socialized.[44] Bronfenbrenner contrasts the Russian method of utilizing children's peer groups as socializing agencies with the American method of assigning the full responsibility for child-rearing to parents and schoolteachers and ignoring the cancelling-out of these influences by asocial peer groups. Since the older the child grows the more time he spends with his peers, the Russian method is more likely to produce the character attributes desired and rewarded by society.

The method used in some Israeli kibbutzim is the same one carried to its logical conclusion. Here the child becomes a resident member of the peer group in infancy when he enters the communal child-rearing facility provided by the village.[45] From that time on he sees his parents for only a few hours a day. The value system of the community is inculcated by nurses, and all of the children internalize it more or less equally. As they get older they take over the sanctioning of behavior.[46] The continuity between the peer group and the adult world plus the spreading of emotional risk among several caretakers reduces the chance of emotional trauma.

Bettelheim, who has studied these youngsters extensively, concludes that "By and large, kibbutz-born youngsters seemed to show considerably less emotional disturbance, both in number of cases and severity, than would a comparable group in the United States."[47] This is a reassuring statement inasmuch as our day care and school arrangements seem to be moving in the direction of the Russian and Israeli models.

School is the child's introduction to the world of formal organizations, and his experience with them is broadened by his subsequent contacts with school teams and clubs. Such activities have often been criticized by taxpayers as educational frills. It may well be, however, that they have important consequences for personality development and social mobility. Interactions within a formal organization provide the child with practice in enacting more impersonal roles than those he plays at home. He observes that the interests and activities of a formal group are more limited and more rationally conceived. The machinery of the organization is clearly visible to him and may be manipulated by any member. The standards of membership in school organizations are the most universalistic that the child has yet encountered. In short, these formal organizations plus the bureaucracy of the school itself provide the child with a rough model of modern society. If he learns to function well in them, they may contribute toward his sense of mastery and his mobility aspirations. If not, he may begin to reject the larger society before he has become a full-fledged member of it.

The relation between organizational membership and mobility has been convincingly demonstrated. People who belong to work-related organizations have consistently lower scores on an attitudinal test of powerlessness than people without such memberships.[48] This is true of both white-collar and blue-collar workers, despite the fact that they may have joined for different reasons. It is especially true of the upwardly mobile in both groups. All of this suggests that satisfactory experience with formal organizations in school may not only help children to outgrow their developmentally and subculturally induced feelings of powerlessness, but may also provide them with an interaction pattern or role-playing style useful for improving their lot in life. A positive experience with formal organizations during the school years might go far toward preventing later alienation from work and from political activities.[49] Developmental psychologists and sociologists could be helpful in building this kind of experience into the school program.

If all of the foregoing tasks are accomplished, then development should proceed at a faster rate, and it may be possible to compress the twelve grades of school into nine or ten. For college-bound youngsters the last two or three years of high school could be combined with college, (an opportunity already being offered by a few colleges), and for the non-college group vocational training with apprenticeships could be provided. This would encourage the developmental advance from Apprentice to Craftsman or Expert, or perhaps even to Faithful Follower or Idealist, thus helping to reduce the tensions of the identity crisis. The school system cannot be expected to carry young people past this plateau, but it could be expected to help them reach it, given conscientious implementation of such a policy. Good vocational counseling would be essential, a counseling based more on developmental and individual characteristics than on IQ and grades. The standardized testing for personality development mentioned earlier would be of great help in the individual's planning for the future. A more vocationally oriented approach to subject matter in the elementary grades and later a systematic presentation of vocational fields would better prepare students for making decisions based upon their testing and counseling.

Economists and governmental administrators will object that a program of cutting down the number of school years would have the effect of flooding the job market in an era when high productivity is eliminating more and more jobs permanently. The answer may lie in the fact that the population is beginning to grow older: i.e., the average age is increasing as the birth rate and death rate continue to drop. The problem could be solved, then, by retiring workers at an earlier age. Those with the personality types of Apprentice and Craftsman-Expert would probably respond with psychosomatic ailments and generalized discontent, as they do to the present retirement arrangements. A public policy oriented toward the developmental welfare of all people might choose to make exceptions of these types and permit them to continue working part-time or periodically as needed in their areas. Those who had reached the Faithful Follower or Faithful Sharer plateaus would be able to accept retirement cooperatively and generously, seeing it as making way for the next generation. The Altruist and Philosopher would accept it joyfully as providing more time for their mature interests. Eventually, if the modal developmental levels of the various social classes rise as predicted and advanced types comprise a higher proportion of the population, the problem will fade away.

The foregoing discussion illustrates the inextricable connections between individual change and structural change. All changes in public policy ultimately produce structural change no matter how individualized the implementing programs may be. Even the most individualized program described here, that of the day care center, will create changes in the institutions of marriage, the family, and child-rearing, if it comes to be provided for all. Clearly it is not only unprofitable to consider one without considering its effects upon the other—it is also unethical. We have no more right to tinker ignorantly with people's lives than doctors have to prescribe medications on a trial-and-error basis. The more power we acquire, the heavier our moral obligations. Thus as action programs proliferate, there will be ever-increasing ethical and practical pressures upon behavioral scientists to provide the soundest possible bases for them. Our reward for the pains of this period will be that having been forced to collect our strength, we shall then be ready to make a quantum leap forward. Beyond it lies a century of achievement which will carry the behavioral sciences to the sophisticated level of the physical sciences.

CONCLUSION

The purpose of this book has been to assemble the evidence from a number of different fields that social class status is positively associated with the level of personality development and thus that the hierarchy of social classes produces a roughly corresponding developmental hierarchy in society. The final chapter has attempted to explore the implications of this theory. The first implication takes the form of a theory of history or of sociocultural development based on Riesman's and Erikson's work. Western culture is seen as moving historically from an early dependence upon traditionalism to a dependence upon rationalism and then toward a neo-humanism which reconciles or synthesizes them. This progression has not only depended upon parallel increases in the modal level(s) of personality development in society but has in turn stimulated further increases. The major trend in Western history, then, has been toward a humanistic society dominated by people of increasingly mature personality types.

The process by which this directionality has been achieved has been the gradual differentiation of institutions out of one another as the functions they performed became specialized. The growth of population, which testifies to the adaptive value of specialization, has put additional pressure behind this trend. A case can be made for the generality of the sequence, for its being applicable to most or all cases of sociocultural development rather than just to our own. The order in which institutions differentiate out seems to be a necessarily fixed one at least up to the point at which the economy is highly rationalized. Then an explosive growth in population is accompanied by a rather explosive institutional differentiation, producing a complex and segmented society.

Given a fixed order of institutional differentiation associated with the fixed order of personality development, the logical tie between them is the modal level of mental operations. The more concrete the typical mentality in a particular society, the less specialization and institutional differentiation will be found in it. At the other end of the scale, the more abstract the typical mentality the more specialization and institutional differentiation will occur—up to a critical level of maturity at which there is a high enough degree of internal control in a high enough proportion of the population to permit society gradually to loosen its external controls. We are probably entering this stage of societal development now. The direct connection between level of personality development and level of societal development suggests that the concept of arrest can apply as well to the latter as to the former. The same caveat applies here, too: it would be just as erroneous to equate primitive man with the modern child as it would be to equate a lower class adult with a middle class child. Personality development is not that simple.

The theory of history presented here yields an optimistic prediction of the future based upon the projection of trends currently in operation. Ironically enough, a major source of opposition to this stance may be the most highly developed group, the neo-humanists. Their pessimism is largely due to the fact that our institutions have not yet been able to adapt to their value-system. Another group is pessimistic because they perceive the beginning of decentralization and the loosening of controls, tendencies which are bound to arouse anxiety in people not developmentally ready for them. In other words the present stage of institutional transition displeases large numbers of people in the new middle class because the rate of change is too slow, and large numbers of old middle and working class people because it is too fast. Only the lower class may find it rather enjoyable. The optimistic prediction is, of course, based on a much longer view than that taken by either group of pessimists. Also it must be qualified by the observation that our society does not exist in a vacuum but in a world full of underdeveloped nations desperately trying to match our economic achievements. Our society's progression to higher modal levels of development may be interrupted at any time by these outside forces.

The second major implication is an activist one. If the main line of reasoning in this view of history is accepted, our obvious course is to encourage personality development by whatever means we can. The first step that suggests itself is a reframing of the national goal in terms of people rather than of things or institutions or even abstract ideals. The second step is to devise appropriate means for implementing this goal. Before effective action can be undertaken, however, the behavioral sciences must work out their common ground, on the basis of which developmental psychology can establish valid norms and reliable testing devices. A growth in the expertise of sociologists and social psychologists is also essential if they are to help officials to design and operate successful policies and programs.

Approaching the problem on the highest structural level, the historico-developmental thesis suggests that the quickest way to get results is by identifying those trends already underway which foster personality development and then by implementing them organizationally. The results of developmental tests performed in connection with programs of this kind could be centrally analyzed so as to provide part of a set of social indicators for measuring society's progress in the desired direction. The successful channeling of social change would give coherence to governmental activities, and the knowledge that it was being channeled directly toward a people-oriented goal would give coherence to the life of the nation.

Because of the critical importance of early childhood for personality development, programs aimed at this period will provide the biggest payoff. Education for parenthood, which at present is sporadic and fractioned, is an obvious place to start. Programs for adults as well as for students could easily be provided by the public schools. For those adults not likely to be reached in this way, television is an excellent means of access. The long-run trend, however, is for governmental policies and programs to bypass parents and concentrate on the provision of day care centers for the rearing of young children.

The public school system's primary purpose is the teaching of cognitive skills, and developmental psychology is already making specific contributions in this area. Cultivating the affective side of personality has been for the most part subordinated or neglected. It is now persuasively argued that this deficiency can be supplied in the elementary grades without introducing new subject matter or compartmentalizing affectivity. One way to accomplish this is by utilizing the comparative-culture materials of the new social science curriculum for affective as well as for cognitive growth. Special teacher training would be necessary, but in any case the thrust of the developmental objective probably requires a rethinking of teacher education. Another way, not yet attempted in this country, is by changing the social structure of the classroom so that the peer group is co-opted by the school system as an agency of moral development. This too would require special teacher training.

The trend toward government's taking on increasing responsibility for the child is most evident in the public school, which must now be concerned with his physical condition, his recreation, and his emotional health, in addition to his cognitive development. The school system takes charge of the child at an increasingly early age and keeps him to a later one, extending the school day and year in order to perform more and more parental functions. Whether or not it continues to move in the direction of the Israeli and Russian models, a concentration upon developing the whole personality along with the teaching skills needed to accomplish this would greatly improve the usefulness and prestige of the public school system. More important still, these changes would increase the average maturity level and in so doing improve the quality of life in our society.

As the reciprocal relationship between structural change and individual change becomes increasingly apparent, so will the moral responsibilities of behavioral scientists. These, added to the practical demands of action programs, will force them to construct a common base and a common language. Once this has been achieved, the behavioral sciences may look forward to a flowering of knowledge and a permanent place in the sun beside the physical sciences.

Notes

Chapter 1

[1]An excellent review of the literature and a cogent discussion of the pitfalls of various approaches to the problem is provided by Edward Zigler in "Social Class and the Socialization Process," *Review of Educational Research 40* (February 1970): 87-110.

[2]For a discussion of these problems see: Thomas E. Lasswell, *Class and Stratum* (Boston: Houghton Mifflin, 1965), pp. 34-67, 473-85; Milton Gordon, *Social Class in American Sociology* (Durham, N.C.: Duke University Press, 1958), in toto.

[3]For an impressive historical tracing of this problem, see John Pease, William H. Form, and Joan Huber Rytina, "Ideological Currents in American Stratification Literature," *American Sociologist 5* (May 1970): 127-37.

[4]For example: W. Lloyd Warner, Marchia Meeker, and Kenneth Eells, *Social Class in America* (Chicago: Science Research Associates, 1949); August Hollingshead and Frederick C. Redlich, *Social Class and Mental Illness* (New York: Wiley & Sons, 1958), pp. 390-7.

[5]Warner, Meeker, and Eells, *Social Class*, p. 168.

[6]Joseph A. Kahl and James A. Davis, "A Comparison of Indexes of Socioeconomic Status," *American Sociological Review 20* (1955): 317-25.

[7]Kurt B. Mayer and Walter Buckley, *Class and Society*, 3d ed. (New York: Random House, 1970), p. 83.

[8]Urie Bronfenbrenner, "Socialization and Social Class Through Time and Space," in Eleanor E. Maccoby, Theodore M. Newcomb, and Eugene L. Hartley, *Readings in Social Psychology*, 3d ed. (New York:

Holt, Rinehart & Winston, 1958), pp. 400-25. See especially p. 405.

[9]Peter M. Blau, "Occupational Bias and Mobility," *American Sociological Review 22* (1957): 392-9.

[10]Richard F. Hamilton, "The Behavior and Values of Skilled Workers," in Arthur B. Shostak and William Gomberg (eds.), *Blue-Collar World* (Englewood Cliffs, N.J.: Prentice-Hall, 1964), pp. 42-57. See especially p. 53.

[11]Richard Centers, *The Psychology of Social Classes* (Princeton, N.J.: Princeton University Press, 1949), p. 100.

[12]Ibid., pp. 95-6.

[13]Ibid., p. 85.

[14]Melvin L. Kohn, "Social Class and Parent-Child Relationships: An Interpretation," *American Journal of Sociology 68* (1963): 471-80.

[15]Seymour M. Lipset and Reinhard Bendix, *Social Mobility in Industrial Society* (Berkeley and Los Angeles: University of California Press, 1959), pp. 14-17.

[16]W. Lloyd Warner, J. O. Low, Paul S. Lunt, and Leo Srole, *Yankee City*, abridged ed. (New Haven: Yale University Press, 1963), pp. 256-62.

[17]W. Lloyd Warner and Paul S. Lunt, *The Social Life of a Modern Community* (New Haven: Yale University Press, 1941), I, p. 85.

[18]Mayer and Buckley, *Class and Society,* p. 84.

[19]Centers, *Psychology of Social Classes*, p. 100.

[20]Hollingshead and Redlich, *Mental Illness*, pp. 390-7.

[21]Michael Harrington, *The Other America* (Baltimore, Md.: Penguin Books, 1962).

[22]Walter B. Miller, "Lower Class Culture as a Generating Milieu of Gang Delinquency," *Journal of Social Issues 14* (1958): 5-19.

[23]Jerome Myers and Bertram Roberts, *Family and Class Dynamics in Mental Illness* (New York: Wiley & Sons, 1959), pp. 49-53.

[24]S. M. Miller, "The American Lower Classes: A Typological Approach." Unpublished paper. (Syracuse, N.Y.: Syracuse University Youth Development Center, 1963), pp. 2 and 4.

[25]Harrington, *The Other America*, p. 9 and Appendix.

[26]The exact figure is 52 percent if only the employed portions of these groups are considered. See *Statistical Abstract of The United States,*

(Washington, D.C.: U. S. Government Printing Office, 1966), Table 323.

[27]Harold L. Wilensky, "Class Consciousness, and American Workers," in Maurice Zeitlin (ed.), *American Society, Inc*. (Chicago: Markham, 1970), pp. 423-37. See especially p. 424.

[28]Constance K. Kamii and Norma L. Radin, "Class Differences in the Socialization Practices of Negro Mothers," *Journal of Marriage and the Family 29* (1967): 302-10; Judith R. Williams and Roland B. Scott, "Growth and Development of Negro Infants: IV. Motor development and Its Relationship to Child Rearing Practices in Two Groups of Negro Infants," *Child Development 24* (June 1953): 103-21; Robert D. Hess and Virginia C. Shipman, "Early Experience and the Socialization of Cognitive Modes in Children," *Child Development 36* (1965): 869-86; Susan Stodolsky and Gerald S. Lesser, "Learning Patterns in the Disadvantaged," in Marcel L. Goldschmid (ed.), *Black Americans and White Racism* (New York: Holt, Rinehart & Winston, 1970), pp. 168-77.

[29]Richard D. Bloom, Martin Whiteman, and Martin Deutsch, "Race and Social Class as Separate Factors," in Martin Deutsch and associates, *The Disadvantaged Child* (New York: Basic Books, 1967), pp. 309-17.

[30]Herbert J. Gans, *The Urban Villagers* (New York: Free Press, 1962), pp. 229-42.

[31]Melvin L. Kohn and Carmi Schooler, "Class, Occupation, and Orientation," *American Sociological Review 34* (1969): 659-78. See footnote on p. 669.

[32]Robin M. Williams, Jr., *American Society* (New York: Knopf, 1959), pp. 129 and 122.

[33]Ibid., pp. 438, 441-1.

[34]Ibid., p. 135.

[35]Ibid., p. 441, f. 105.

[36]Ibid., pp. 441-2.

[37]S. M. Miller and Frank Riessman, "The Working Class Subculture: A New View," *Social Problems 9* (Summer 1961): 86-97. Cf. the "routine-seekers" in Gans, *The Urban Villagers*, pp. 28-31, discussed at the end of this chapter.

[38]Richard Hoggart, *The Uses of Literacy* (London: Penguin Books, Chatto and Windus, 1959).

[39]Ibid., pp. 15-20.

[40]Ibid., p. 19.

[41]Ibid., pp. 20-41.

[42]Ibid., pp. 41-52.

[43]Ibid., Chapter 3.

[44]Ibid., pp. 79-87.

[45]Ibid., pp. 105-12.

[46]Albert K. Cohen and Harold M. Hodges, Jr., "Characteristics of the Lower-Blue-Collar Class," *Social Problems 10* (Spring 1963): 303-34.

[47]Edward Zigler and Irvin L. Child, "Intrasocietal Variation in Socialization," in Gardner Lindzey and Elliot Aronson (eds.), *The Handbook of Social Psychology*, 2d ed. (Reading, Mass.: Addison-Wesley, 1969), III, pp. 483-501.

[48]Henry W. Maier, *Three Theories of Child Development* (New York: Harper & Row, 1965), p. 3.

[49]Ibid.

[50]Ibid., p. 91; John H. Flavell, *The Developmental Psychology of Jean Piaget* (Princeton, N.J.: Van Nostrand, 1963), pp. 19-20.

[51]Maier, *Three Theories*, pp. 30-51.

[52]Heinz Werner, "The Concept of Development from a Comparative and Organismic Point of View," in Dale Harris (ed.), *The Concept of Development* (Minneapolis: University of Minnesota Press, 1957), pp. 125-48. See p. 127.

[53]Elton B. McNeil, "Conceptual and Motoric Expressiveness in Two Social Classes," *Dissertation Abstracts 13* (1953): 437.

[54]H. A. Witkin, H. B. Lewis, M. Hertzman, K. Machover, P. Bretnall Meissner, and S. Wapman, *Personality Through Perception* (New York: Harper, 1954).

[55]O.J. Harvey, David E. Hunt, and Harold M. Schroder, *Conceptual Systems and Personality Organization* (New York: Wiley & Sons, 1961).

[56]Julian B. Rotter, Melvin Seeman, and Shephard Liverant, "Internal versus External Control of Reinforcements: A Major Variable in Behavior Theory," in Norman F. Washburne (ed.), *Decisions, Values and Groups* (London: Pergamon Press, 1962), II, pp. 473-516.

[57]Flavell, *Jean Piaget*, p. 203.

[58]Ibid., pp. 203-4.

[59]Ibid., pp. 204-6.

[60]Maier, *Three Theories*, pp. 65-7.

[61]Werner, "Concept of Development," p. 127.

[62]Talcott Parsons, *The Social System* (Glencoe, Ill.: Free Press, 1951), p. 62.

[63]Williams, *American Society*, p. 435.

[64]Gans, *The Urban Villagers*, pp. 28-31.

[65]Ibid., p. 30.

[66]Ibid., p. 29.

Chapter 2

[1]Jane E. Brody, "It Really May be 'Food for Thought'," *New York Times* (July 28, 1968), p. 10 E.

[2]Ibid.

[3]Ibid.

[4]"Malnutrition and Brain Damage," *Science News 99* (April 17, 1971): 266. (Experimental study performed on rats.)

[5]David Krech, "The Chemistry of Learning," *Saturday Review 51* (January 20, 1968): 50.

[6]"Environment Important," *Science News 90* (October 1, 1966): 248.

[7]"An Earlier Head Start," *Science News 100* (July 10, 1971): 24; Rick F. Heber and Richard B. Dever, "Research on Education and Habilitation of the Mentally Retarded," in H. Carl Haywood (ed.), *Social-Cultural Aspects of Mental Retardation* (New York: Meredith Corp. of Appleton-Century-Crofts, 1970), pp. 395-427. See especially pp. 419-21. The material in this first section of Chapter 2 should help to discredit the new wave of genetic determinism: e.g., Arthur R. Jensen, "How Much Can We Boost IQ and Scholastic Achievement?" *Harvard Educational Review 39* (Winter 1969): 13-16; Richard Herrnstein, "IQ," *Atlantic 228* (September 1971): 43-58ff.

[8]Dr. Robert Cook, chief of pediatrics at Johns Hopkins Medical Center in Baltimore is quoted in *Time 99* (May 8, 1972): 52 as saying "While genetic, chromosomal and hereditary causes occur with the same frequency in all racial and economic groups, retardation of unknown origin is nearly ten times more likely to occur among the poor, black and

Spanish-speaking in the U.S. than among the white and affluent." The term "of unknown origin" includes all of the factors mentioned in this section and probably others as well.

[9]Maya Pines, "Why Some 3-Year-Olds Get A's—And Some Get C's," *New York Times Magazine* (July 6, 1969): 4 ff. A full report of the Harvard Pre-School Project's findings is to be made in Burton L. White et al., *Experience and Environment: Major Influences on the Development of the Young Child* (Englewood Cliffs, N.J.: Prentice-Hall, 1973).

[10]Pines, "Why Some 3-Year-Olds," p. 10.

[11]Ibid., p. 12.

[12]Ibid., p. 15.

[13]Ibid.

[14]James Walters, Ruth Connor, and Michael Zunich, "Interaction of Mothers and Children from Lower-Class Families," *Child Development* 35 (1964): 433-40.

[15]Ibid.

[16]Elizabeth Bing, "Effect of Childrearing Practices on Development of Differential Cognitive Abilities," *Child Development 34* (1963): 631-48.

[17]Dorothea McCarthy, "Language Development in the Child," in Leonard Carmichael (ed.), *Manual of Child Psychology* (New York: Wiley & Sons, 1954), pp. 492-630. See especially pp. 586-8.

[18]Andrew J. Schwebel, "Effects of Impulsivity on Performance of Verbal Tasks in Middle- and Lower-Class Children," *American Journal of Orthopsychiatry 36* (1966): 13-21.

[19]Donald C. Findlay and Carson McGuire, "Social Status and Abstract Behavior," *Journal of Abnormal and Social Psychology 54* (1957): 135-7. Intelligence was controlled. Vera P. John, "The Intellectual Development of Slum Children: Some Preliminary Findings," *American Journal of Orthopsychiatry 33* (1963): 813-22.

[20]Eugene S. Gollin, "Organizational Characteristics of Social Judgment: A Developmental Investigation," *Journal of Personality 26* (1958): 139-54. Intelligence was controlled.

[21]David E. Hunt and John Dopyera, "Personality Variation in Lower-Class Children," *Journal of Psychology 62* (1966): 47-54. About 75 percent of the lower class children were black. Jerome Siller,

"Socioeconomic Status and Conceptual Thinking," *Journal of Abnormal and Social Psychology 55* (1957): 365-71.

[22]Robert D. Hess and Virginia C. Shipman, "Early Experience and the Socialization of Cognitive Modes in Children," *Child Development 36* (1965): 869-86; John, "Intellectual Development of Slum Children"; Hunt and Dopyera, "Personality Variation;" examines two racial groups.

[23]William R. Rosengren, "Social Status, Attitudes Toward Pregnancy and Child-Rearing Attitudes," *Social Forces 41* (1962): 127-34.

[24]Ibid.

[25]Martin L. Hoffman, "Power Assertion by the Parent and Its Impact on the Child," *Child Development 31* (1960): 129-43; Martin L. Hoffman, "Parent Discipline and the Child's Consideration for Others," *Child Development 35* (1963): 573-88.

[26]Hoffman, "Parent Discipline."

[27]Constance K. Kamii and Norma L. Radin, "Class Differences in the Socialization Practices of Negro Mothers," *Journal of Marriage and the Family 29* (1967): 302-10.

[28]Robert D. Hess, "Educability and Rehabilitation: The Future of the Welfare Class," *Journal of Marriage and the Family 26* (1964): 422-29.

[29]"Culture Molds the Brain," *Science News 95* (January 18, 1969): 61.

[30]Ibid.; the language is that of Dr. Robert Livingstone of the University of California at San Diego.

[31]Basil Bernstein, "Some Sociological Determinants of Perception," *British Journal of Sociology 9* (1958): 159-74.

[32]Ibid.

[33]Ibid.

[34]Basil Bernstein, "A Public Language: Some Sociological Implications of a Linguistic Form," *British Journal of Sociology 10* (1959): 311-26.

[35]Ibid.

[36]Frank Riessman, *The Culturally Deprived Child* (New York: Harper, 1962), p. 76.

[37]Bernstein, "A Public Language."

[38]Bernstein, "Sociological Determinants."

[39]Bernstein, "A Public Language."

[40]Bernstein, "Sociological Determinants."

[41]Ibid.

[42]Bernstein, "A Public Language."

[43]Walter B. Miller, "Lower Class Culture as a Generating Milieu of Gang Delinquency," *Journal of Social Issues 14* (1958): 5-19.

[44]Riessman, *The Culturally Deprived Child*, p. 73.

[45]Leonard Schatzman and Anselm Strauss, "Social Class and Modes of Communication," *American Journal of Sociology 60* (1955): 329-38.

[46]Joseph Church, *Language and the Discovery of Reality* (New York: Random House, 1961), p. 26.

[47]Schatzman and Strauss, "Modes of Communication."

[48]Ibid.

[49]Bernstein, "A Public Language."

[50]Schatzman and Strauss, "Modes of Communication."

[51]Ibid.

[52]Bernstein, "A Public Language."

[53]Hess, "Educability and Rehabilitation."

[54]Judith R. Williams and Roland B. Scott, "Growth and Development of Negro Infants: IV. Motor Development and Its Relationship to Child Rearing Practices in Two Groups of Negro Infants," *Child Development 24* (1953): 103-21.

[55]Howard A. Moss, Kenneth S. Robson, and Frank Pedersen, "Determinants of Maternal Stimulation of Infants and Consequences of Treatment for Later Reactions to Strangers," *Developmental Psychology 1* (1969): 239-46.

[56]Elton B. McNeil, "Conceptual and Motoric Expressiveness in Two Social Classes," *Dissertation Abstracts 13* (1953): 437.

[57]Daniel R. Miller and Guy E. Swanson, *Inner Conflict and Defense* (New York: Henry Holt, 1960): pp. 341-54.

[58]Ibid., p. 348.

[59]Ibid., pp. 341-2.

[60]Ibid., pp. 344 and 346.

[61]Bernstein, "Sociological Determinants."

[62]Miller and Swanson, *Inner Conflict*, pp. 350-2.

[63]H. A. Witkin, H. B. Lewis, M. Hertzman, K. Machover, P. Bretnall

Meissner, and S. Wapman, *Personality Through Perception* (New York: Harper, 1954), pp. 25-37.

[64]Ibid., p. 23.

[65]Ibid., p. 151.

[66]Ibid., pp. 36-7.

[67]Henry W. Maier, *Three Theories of Child Development* (New York: Harper & Row, 1965), pp. 135-41; Richard M. Jones, *Fantasy and Feeling in Education* (New York: New York University Press, 1968), pp. 130-1.

[68]H.A. Witkin, R. B. Dyk, H. F. Faterson, D. R. Goodenough, and S. A. Karp, *Psychological Differentiation* (New York: Wiley & Sons, 1962), p. 3.

[69]Ibid., p. 5.

[70]Ibid., pp. 3-4.

[71]Witkin, et al., *Personality Through Perception*, p. 498.

[72]Ibid., p. 479.

[73]Robert C. Misch, "The Relationship of Motoric Inhibition to Developmental Level and Ideational Functioning: An Analysis by Means of the Rorschach Test," *Dissertation Abstracts 14* (1954): 1810-11.

[74]Ibid.

[75]David Massari, Lois Hayweiser, and William J. Meyer, "Activity Level and Intellectual Functioning in Deprived Preschool Children," *Developmental Psychology 1* (1969): 286-90.

[76]See also: Jerome Kagan, "Reflection-Impulsivity and Reading Ability in Primary Grade Children," *Child Development 36* (1965): 609-28; Jerome Kagan, Leslie Pearson and Lois Welch, "Conceptual Impulsivity and Inductive Reasoning," *Child Development 37* (1966): 583-94.

[77]Schwebel, "Effects of Impulsivity."

[78]Formulation based on that of George Herbert Mead in Charles W. Morris (ed.), *Mind, Self, and Society* (Chicago: University of Chicago Press, 1934), pp. 152-64.

[79]Melvin H. Feffer, "The Cognitive Implications of Role-Taking Behavior," *Journal of Personality 27* (1959): 152-68.

[80]Ibid.

[81]Melvin H. Feffer, "Cognitive Aspects of Role-Taking in Children," *Journal of Personality 28* (1960): 383-96.

[82]Feffer "Implications."

[83]Raymond Wolfe, "The Role of Conceptual Systems in Cognitive Functioning at Varying Levels of Age and Intelligence," *Journal of Personality 31* (1963): 108-23.

[84]Norman Milgram and Harold Goodglass, "Role Style versus Cognitive Maturation in Word Associations of Adults and Children," *Journal of Personality 29* (1961): 81-93.

[85]Schatzman and Strauss, "Modes of Communication."

[86]Julienne Ford, Douglas Young, and Steven Box, "Functional Autonomy, Role Distance, and Social Class," *British Journal of Sociology 18* (1967): 370-81.

[87]Herbert Gans, *The Urban Villagers* (Glencoe, Ill.: Free Press, 1962), p. 102.

Chapter 3

[1]Jean Piaget, *The Moral Judgment of the Child* (Glencoe, Ill.: Free Press, 1932), pp. 192-4, 312-25.

[2]Robert W. White, "Ego and Reality in Psychoanalytic Theory," *Psychological Issues III*, Monograph 11 (1963): 111.

[3]Albert D. Ullman, "Identification: An Interactionist Interpretation." Unpublished paper. (Medford, Mass.: Tufts University, 1954); White, "Ego and Reality," pp. 95-124.

[4]George Herbert Mead in Chester W. Morris (ed.), *Mind, Self, and Society* (Chicago: University of Chicago Press, 1934), pp. 135-44, 192-200.

[5]Ullman, "Identification"; White, "Ego and Reality," pp. 111-13.

[6]White, "Ego and Reality," p. 112.

[7]Robert H. Sears, Eleanor E. Maccoby, and Harry Levin, *Patterns of Child Rearing* (Evanston, Ill.: Row, Peterson, 1957), p. 375.

[8]Ferdynand Zweig, *The British Worker* (Baltimore, Md.: Penguin Books, 1952), pp. 64-5.

[9]Albert Bandura and Richard H. Walters, *Adolescent Aggression* (New York: Ronald Press, 1959), 354-5; Herbert Gans, *The Urban Villagers* (Glencoe, Ill.: Free Press, 1962), p. 64.

[10]Jerome Myers and Bertram Roberts, *Family and Class Dynamics in Mental Illness* (New York: Wiley & Sons, 1959), p. 260.

[11]Piaget, *Moral Judgment*.

[12]Lawrence Kohlberg, "Development of Moral Character and Moral Ideology," in Martin L. and Lois W. Hoffman, *Review of Child Development Research* (New York: Russell Sage Foundation, 1964), I, pp. 383-431. See especially p. 395.

[13]Ibid., p. 400.

[14]Ibid., pp. 404 and 406.

[15]Ibid., pp. 412-13.

[16]Ibid.

[17]Lee Rainwater, Richard P. Coleman, and Gerald Handel, *Workingman's Wife* (New York: Oceana Publications, 1950), pp. 91-3; Gans, *The Urban Villagers*, p. 59; Carson McGuire, "Family Life in Lower and Middle Class Homes," *Marriage and Family Living 14* (1952): 1-6; Melvin L. Kohn, "Social Class and the Exercise of Parental Authority," *American Sociological Review 24* (1959): 352-66.

[18]Piaget, *Moral Judgment*, p. 26.

[19]Gans, *The Urban Villagers*, p. 59.

[20]Rainwater, et al., *Workingman's Wife*, pp. 93-4.

[21]Henry Maas, "Some Social Class Differences in the Family Systems and Group Relations of Pre- and Early Adolescents," *Child Development 22* (1951): 145-52; Robert J. Havighurst mentions a study with similar results in "Social Class and Basic Personality Structure," *Sociology and Social Research 36* (1952): 355-63.

[22]McGuire, "Family Life."

[23]Rainwater, et al., *Workingman's Wife*, p. 70.

[24]Melvin L. Kohn and Eleanor E. Carroll, "Social Class and the Allocation of Parental Responsibilities," *Sociometry 23* (1960): 372-92.

[25]Glen H. Elder, Jr. and Charles E. Bowerman, "Family Structure and Child-Rearing Patterns: The Effect of Family Size and Sex Composition," *American Sociological Review 28* (1963): 891-905.

[26]Ibid.

[27]Glen H. Elder, Jr., "Structural Variations in the Child-Rearing Relationship," *Sociometry 25* (1962): 241-62; Urie Bronfenbrenner finds this trend toward middle class equalitarianism confirmed in the

studies he has collated in "Socialization and Social Class Through Time and Space," in Eleanor E. Maccoby, Theodore M. Newcomb, and Eugene L. Hartley (eds.), *Readings in Social Psychology* 3rd ed. (New York: Holt, Rinehart & Winston, 1958), pp. 420-21.

[28]Marian R. Winterbottom, "The Relation of Need for Achievement to Learning Experiences in Independence and Mastery," in John W. Atkinson (ed.), *Motives in Fantasy, Action, and Society* (Princeton, N.J.: Van Nostrand, 1958), pp. 453-78; Allison Davis and Robert J. Havighurst, "Social Class and Color Differences in Child-Rearing," *American Sociological Review 11* (1946): 698-710; Martha Ericson, "Child Rearing and Social Status," in Theodore M. Newcomb and Eugene L. Hartley (eds.), *Readings in Social Psychology* (New York: Holt, 1947), pp. 494-501.

[29]Robert J. Havighurst and Allison Davis, "A Comparison of the Chicago and Harvard Studies of Social Class Differences in Child-Rearing," *American Sociological Review 20* (1955): 438-42.

[30]Sears, et al., *Patterns of Child Rearing*, p. 430.

[31]Bronfenbrenner, "Socialization and Social Class," p. 415.

[32]Ibid.

[33]Urie Bronfenbrenner, "Some Familial Antecedents of Responsibility and Leadership in Adolescents," in Luigi Petrullo and Bernard Bass (eds.), *Leadership and Interpersonal Behavior* (New York: Holt, Rinehart & Winston, 1961), pp. 239-71.

[34]Ibid., pp. 254-5. Father's education was used as the indicator of social class level.

[35]Ibid., p. 255.

[36]Gans, *The Urban Villagers*, p. 87.

[37] Ibid., p. 99.

[38]Robert E. Stoltz and Marshall D. Smith, "Some Effects of Socio-Economic, Age and Sex Factors on Children's Responses to the Rosenzweig Picture-Frustration Study," *Journal of Clinical Psychology 15* (1959): 200-3.

[39]Kohlberg, "Development of Moral Character," pp. 406-7.

[40]Sears, et al., *Patterns of Child Rearing*, p. 386. They also consider identification with parents to be an important factor in the development of conscience: pp. 368-76.

[41]Ibid., p. 388.

[42]Ibid., p. 31; Bronfenbrenner, "Socialization and Social Class," pp. 418-9.

[43]Martin L. Hoffman and Herbert D. Saltzstein, "Parent Discipline and the Child's Moral Development," *Journal of Personality and Social Psychology 5* (1967): 45-57. This is one of the studies which gives no explanation of the criteria of "lower class" or "middle class."

[44]Duncan MacRae, Jr., "A Test of Piaget's Theories of Moral Development," *Journal of Abnormal and Social Psychology 49* (1954): 14-18.

[45]Bronfenbrenner, "Familial Antecedents," pp. 249-50.

[46]The only study found which did not give evidence of social class differences in moral development is that of Leonore Boehm and Martin L. Nass, "Social Class Differences in Conscience Development," *Child Development 33* (1962): 565-74. The method used in this study was to classify children's reactions to four stories in terms of their responses representing one of Piaget's three stages of moral development. The children were 160 first through sixth graders in the public schools, all with IQ's of 90 and above. On the basis of the father's occupation, roughly half were judged to be working class and the other half upper middle class. Significant age differentials in moral development were found, as expected, but the investigators reported finding no significant social class differences.

This negative result turns out to be due to the dichotomizing of moral development into Stages 1-plus-2 and Stage 3. When the data are reconstructed (the raw data are not given) and the chi squares are calculated for *three* levels of development in the two social class groups, they show significant class differences beyond the .02 level in the expected direction for three out of the four test stories. The fourth does not present a moral issue, and in fact the investigators expected to find no social class difference here. Why they should have thrown away the significant breakdown on the other three stories is a mystery, unless it was for ideological reasons to avoid the unpalatable conclusion that the working class children showed a lower or slower moral development than the middle class children.

[47]Julian B. Rotter, Melvin Seeman, and Shephard Liverant, "Internal

versus External Control of Reinforcements: A Major Variable in Behavior Theory," in Norman F. Washburne (ed.), *Decisions, Values and Groups* (London: Pergamon Press, 1962), II, pp. 473-516.

[48]Julian B. Rotter, "Generalized Expectancies for Internal versus External Control of Reinforcements," *Psychological Monographs 80*, Monograph 609 (1966).

[49]Irv Bialer, "Conceptualization of Success and Failure in Mentally Retarded and Normal Children," *Journal of Personality 29* (1961): 303-20.

[50]Esther Battle and Julian B. Rotter, "Children's Feelings of Personal Control as Related to Social Class and Ethnic Group," *Journal of Personality 31* (1963): 482-90.

[51]Elias Tuma and Norman Livson, "Family Socioeconomic Status and Adolescent Attitudes Toward Authority," *Child Development 31* (1960): 387-99.

[52]Theodore D. Graves, "Time Perspective and the Deferred Gratification Pattern in a Tri-Ethnic Community," Research Report #5, Tri-Ethnic Research Project, University of Colorado, Boulder, Colorado (1961): 51-3.

[53]Ibid., pp. 66-9.

[54]Ibid., pp. 123, 178, and 269.

[55]Justin Aronfreed, *Conduct and Conscience* (New York: Academic Press, 1968), p. 326.

[56]Ibid., pp. 326-8.

[57]Ibid., pp. 261-2; Kohlberg, "Moral Character," p. 406.

[58]Melvin Wallace and Albert I. Rabin, "Temporal Experience," *Psychological Bulletin 57* (1960): 213-36.

[59]Heinz Werner, "The Concept of Development from a Comparative and Organismic Point of View," in Dale Harris (ed.), *The Concept of Development* (Minneapolis: University of Minnesota Press, 1957), p. 127.

[60]Lawrence L. LeShan, "Time Orientation and Social Class," *Journal of Abnormal and Social Psychology 47* (1952): 589-92. This includes a review of the literature.

[61]Robert D. Hess and Virginia C. Shipman, "Early Experience and the Socialization of Cognitive Modes in Children," *Child Development 36* (1965): 869-86.

[62]LeShan, "Time Orientation."

[63]Ibid.

[64]J.E. Greene and A. H. Roberts, "Time Orientation and Social Class: A Correction," *Journal of Abnormal and Social Psychology 62* (1961): 141.

[65]Graves, "Time Perspective," p. 24.

[66]Louis Schneider and Sverre Lysgaard, "The Deferred Gratification Pattern: A Preliminary Study," *American Sociological Review 18* (1953): 142-9.

[67]Murray A. Straus, "Deferred Gratification, Social Class, and the Achievement Syndrome," *American Sociological Review 27* (1962): 326-35.

[68]Harry Beilin, "The Pattern of Postponability and Its Relation to Social Class Mobility," *Journal of Social Psychology 44* (1956): 33-48.

[69]Robert F. Peck and Robert J. Havighurst, *The Psychology of Character Development* (New York: Wiley & Sons, 1960).

[70]Ibid., p. 3.

[71]Ibid., p. 5.

[72]Ibid., p. 6.

[73]Ibid.

[74]Ibid, p. 7.

[75]Ibid.

[76]Ibid., p. 9.

[77]Ibid.

[78]Ibid., pp. 170-3.

[79]Ibid., pp. 176-7.

[80]Ibid., p. 185.

[81]Ibid.

[82]Ibid., p. 183.

Chapter 4

[1]Elizabeth Bott, *Family and Social Network* (London: Tavistock Publications, 1957), pp. 53-4; Gans cites Bott's description of British working class people as applying equally to their American counterparts:

Herbert Gans, *The Urban Villagers* (Glencoe, Ill.: Free Press, 1962), p. 50.

[2]Gans, *The Urban Villagers*, p. 48.

[3]Ibid., pp. 50-2.

[4]Ibid., p. 51.

[5]Armand A. Alkire, "Social Power and Communication Within Families of Disturbed and Nondisturbed Adolescents," *Journal of Personality and Social Psychology 13* (1969): 335-49.

[6]Murray A. Straus, "Communication, Creativity, and Problem-Solving Ability of Middle- and Working-Class Families in Three Societies," *American Journal of Sociology 73* (1968): 417-30.

[7]Lee Rainwater, "Marital Sexuality in Four Cultures of Poverty," *Journal of Marriage and the Family 26* (1964): 457-66.

[8]Lee Rainwater, *And the Poor Get Children* (Chicago: Quadrangle Books, 1960), pp. x-xi.

[9]Gans, *The Urban Villagers*, p. 49.

[10]Rainwater, "Marital Sexuality."

[11]Robert O. Blood, Jr. and Donald M. Wolfe, *Husbands and Wives* (Glencoe, Ill.: Free Press, 1960), pp. 228-9; Kinsey's study *Sexual Behavior in the Human Female*, as quoted by Rainwater, *And the Poor*, pp. x-xi, also found education to be the differentiating factor.

[12]Rainwater, *And the Poor*, p. 26, quotes Freedman, Whelpton and Campbell's *Family Planning, Sterility, and Population Growth* (1959) to this effect.

[13]Rainwater, *And the Poor*, pp. 144-5.

[14]August B. Hollingshead, "Class Differences in Family Stability," in Reinhard Bendix and Seymour Lipset (eds.), *Class, Status, and Power* (Glencoe, Ill.: Free Press, 1953), pp. 284-92. See especially pp. 290-1.

[15]J. Richard Udry, "Marital Instability by Race and Income Based on 1960 Census Data," *American Journal of Sociology 72* (1967): 673-4. He also found an inverse relationship between social class and marital disruption when occupation and education were used as separate indicators of social class. Udry, "Marital Instability by Race, Sex, Education, and Occupation Using 1960 Census Data," *American Journal of Sociology 72* (1967): 203-9.

[16]William J. Goode, *After Divorce* (Glencoe, Ill.: Free Press, 1956),

p. 44 and Chapter IV generally, pp. 43-55. Chapter V, pp. 57-68, discusses the meaning of the class differentials in divorce rates.

[17]Gans, *The Urban Villagers*, p. 53. This is also occurring in England, according to Ferdynand Zweig in *The Worker in an Affluent Society* (Glencoe, Ill.: Free Press, 1961), pp. 32 and 208.

[18]Gerald Handel and Lee Rainwater, "Persistence and Change in Working Class Life Style." Unpublished paper. (Chicago: Social Research, Inc., 1963).

[19]Lee Rainwater and Gerald Handel, "Changing Family Roles in the Working Class." Unpublished paper. (Chicago: Social Research, Inc., 1963).

[20]The literature is reviewed by S. M. Miller and Frank Riessman, "The Working Class Subculture: A New View," *Social Problems 9* (1961): 86-97; Gans, *The Urban Villagers*, pp. 37 and 46; Bert N. Adams, *Kinship in an Urban Setting* (Chicago: Markham, 1968), pp. 30-2, 164-8.

[21]Bennett M. Berger, *Working-Class Suburb* (Los Angeles: University of California Press, 1960), p. 68.

[22]Lee Rainwater, Richard P. Coleman, and Gerald Handel, *Workingman's Wife* (New York: Oceana Publications, 1950), p. 104.

[23]Albert K. Cohen and Harold M. Hodges, Jr., "Characteristics of the Lower-Blue-Collar Class," *Social Problems 10* (1963): 303-34.

[24]Marvin B. Sussman, "The Isolated Nuclear Family: Fact or Fiction," *Social Problems 6* (1959): 333-40; Berger, *Working-Class Suburb*, p. 68; Cohen and Hodges, "Lower-Blue-Collar Class"; Adams, *Kinship*, pp. 30-1.

[25]Joseph A. Kahl, *The American Class Structure* (New York: Holt, Rinehart & Winston, 1957), pp. 137-8.

[26]Berger, *Working-Class Suburb*, p. 67.

[27]Ibid., p. 70.

[28]Rainwater, et al., *Workingman's Wife*, p. 116; Zweig, *The Worker*, p. 104.

[29]Cohen and Hodges, "Lower-Blue-Collar Class."

[30]Robert Dubin, "Industrial Workers' Worlds: A Study of the 'Central Life Interests' of Industrial Workers," in Arnold M. Rose (ed.), *Human Behavior and Social Process* (Boston: Houghton Mifflin, 1962), pp. 247-66. See especially p. 249.

[31]Morris Axelrod, "Urban Structure and Social Participation," *American Sociological Review 21* (1956): 13-18; Cohen and Hodges, "Lower-Blue-Collar Class"; Zweig, *The Worker*, pp. 82 and 117.

[32]John C. Glidewell, Mildred B. Kantor, Louis M. Smith, and Lorene A. Stringer, "Socialization and Social Structure in the Classroom," in Lois W. and Martin L. Hoffman (eds.), *Review of Child Development Research* (New York: Russell Sage Foundation, 1966), II, pp. 221-56. See especially pp. 235-7. Also the following: Elizabeth Douvan and Martin Gold, "Modal Patterns in American Adolescence," in Hoffman and Hoffman, *Review,* II, pp. 469-528, especially pp. 493 and 495; Margaret J. Lundberg, "The Reciprocated Best Friendship Choices of College Women." Unpublished thesis. (Medford, Mass.: Tufts University, 1961). See especially the review of the literature.

[33]Glidewell, et al., "Socialization," p. 241; Lundberg, "Best Friendship"; Kahl, *American Class Structure*, pp. 129-36.

[34]Wendell Bell and Maryanne T. Force, "Urban Neighborhood Types and Participation in Formal Associations," *American Sociological Review 21* (1956), 25-34; Mirra Komarovsky, "The Voluntary Associations of Urban Dwellers," *American Sociological Review 11* (1946): 686-98; Leonard Reissman, "Class, Leisure, and Social Participation," *American Sociological Review 19* (1954): 76-84; Charles R. Wright and Herbert H. Hyman, "Voluntary Association Memberships of American Adults: Evidence from National Surveys," *American Sociological Review 23* (1958): 284-94, a summary of a number of representative sample surveys.

[35]Murray Hausknecht, "The Blue-Collar Joiner," in Arthur B. Shostak and William Gomberg (eds.), *Blue-Collar World* (Englewood Cliffs, N.J.: Prentice-Hall, 1964), pp. 207-15. See especially p. 207.

[36]Axelrod, "Urban Structure."

[37]Floyd Dotson, "Patterns of Voluntary Association Among Urban Working-Class Families," *American Sociological Review 16* (1951): 687-93.

[38]Jerome Myers and Bertram Roberts, *Family and Class Dynamics in Mental Illness* (New York: Wiley & Sons, 1959), pp. 49-53.

[39]Arthur Kornhauser, Harold L. Sheppard, and Albert J. Mayer, *When Labor Votes* (New York: University Books, 1956), p. 28.

[40]Bell and Force, "Urban Neighborhood Types."

[41]Komarovsky, "Voluntary Associations"; Myers and Roberts, *Family and Class Dynamics*, pp. 49-53.

[42]Dotson, "Voluntary Association."

[43]Hausknecht, "Blue-Collar Joiner," p. 210.

[44]Axelrod, "Urban Structure"; Bell and Force, "Urban Neighborhood Types"; Riessman, "Class, Leisure."

[45]Frank Riessman, "Workers' Attitudes Toward Participation and Leadership," *Dissertation Abstracts 15* (1955): 1923-4.

[46]Rainwater, et al., *Workingman's Wife,* p. 20.

[47]Riessman, "Workers' Attitudes."

[48]Cohen and Hodges, "Lower-Blue-Collar Class."

[49]Dubin, "Industrial Workers' Worlds," p. 259.

[50]Ibid., pp. 248 and 252.

[51]Ibid., p. 263; Gans, *The Urban Villagers*, p. 124.

[52]Nancy C. Morse and Robert S. Weiss, "The Function and Meaning of Work and the Job," *American Sociological Review 20* (1955): 191-8.

[53]William Erbe, "Social Involvement and Political Activity: A Replication and Elaboration," *American Sociological Review 29* (1964): 198-215; Marvin E. Olsen, "Social Participation and Voting Turnout: A Multivariate Analysis," *American Sociological Review 37* (1972): 317-33.

[54]Richard M. Scammon and Ben J. Wattenberg, *The Real Majority* (New York: Coward-McCann, 1970), p. 54.

[55]Seymour M. Lipset, *Political Man* (Garden City, N.Y.: Doubleday, 1960), p. 184; Hugh A. Bone and Austin Ranney, *Politics and Voters* (New York: McGraw-Hill, 1963), pp. 20 and 31.

[56]Erbe, "Social Involvement."

[57]Margherita MacDonald, Carson McGuire, and Robert J. Havighurst, "Leisure Activities and the Socioeconomic Status of Children," *American Journal of Sociology 54* (1949): 505-19.

[58]Gans, *The Urban Villagers*, p. 37.

[59]Ibid., p. 38.

[60]Leon Festinger, *A Theory of Cognitive Dissonance* (Evanston, Ill.: Row, Peterson, 1957).

[61]Leonard Broom and Philip Selznick, *Sociology* 4th edition (New York: Harper & Row, 1968), p. 179, based on data from Herbert P. Miller, *Income of the American People* (New York: Wiley & Sons,

1955), pp. 31-3. See also Kahl, *American Class Structure*, pp. 129-36.

[62]The use of identification as a means of improving oneself has been empirically demonstrated in Lundberg, "Best Friendship."

Chapter 5

[1]O. J. Harvey, David E. Hunt, and Harold M. Schroder, *Conceptual Systems and Personality Organization* (New York: Wiley & Sons, 1961), pp. 50 and 55.

[2]Ibid., pp. 24-6.

[3]Ibid., p. 19.

[4]Ibid., pp. 91, 114-15.

[5]Ibid., p. 115.

[6]Ibid., p. 170.

[7]Ibid., pp. 94-7.

[8]Ibid., pp. 94-5.

[9]"Reliable Unilateral Training." Ibid., pp. 121, 127, 135.

[10]"Accelerated Unilateral Training." Ibid., pp. 150, 175-6.

[11]Ibid., pp. 98-101.

[12]"Unreliable Unilateral Training." Ibid., pp. 128-9, 135-6.

[13]Ibid., pp. 128-9.

[14]"Accelerated Autonomous Training." Ibid., pp. 151-2.

[15]Ibid., pp. 106-9.

[16]Ibid. pp. 101-6.

[17]Ibid., pp. 101-3.

[18]"Protective Interdependent Training." Ibid., pp. 129-30.

[19]Ibid., p. 137.

[20]"Accelerated Interdependent Training." Ibid., pp. 152.

[21]"Informational Interdependent Training." Ibid., pp. 130-2.

[22]T. W. Adorno, Else Frenkel-Brunswik, Daniel J. Levinson, and R. Nevitt Sanford, *The Authoritarian Personality* (New York: Harper & Row, 1950), pp. 255-7.

[23]Else Frenkel-Brunswik, "Further Explorations by a Contributor to *The Authoritarian Personality*," in Richard Christie and Marie Jahoda

(eds.), *Studies in the Scope and Method of "The Authoritarian Personality"* (Glencoe, Ill.: Free Press, 1954), pp. 226-75. See especially p. 273.

[24]Milton Rokeach, "Generalized Mental Rigidity as a Factor in Ethnocentrism," *Journal of Abnormal and Social Psychology 43* (1948): 259-78.

[25]Irvin J. Lehmann, "Some Socio-Cultural Differences in Attitudes and Values," *Journal of Educational Sociology 36* (1962): 1-9.

[26]Adorno, et al., *The Authoritarian Personality*, pp. 482-3.

[27]Ibid. p. 455.

[28]Julian B. Rotter, Melvin Seeman, and Shephard Liverant, "Internal versus External Control of Reinforcements: A Major Variable in Behavior Theory," in Norman F. Washburne (ed.), *Decisions, Values and Groups* (London: Pergamon Press, 1962), II, pp. 473-516.

[29]Seymour M. Lipset, *Political Man* (Garden City, N.Y.: Doubleday, 1960), pp. 97-130.

[30]S. M. Miller and Frank Riessman, "The Working Class Subculture: A New View," *Social Problems 9* (1961): 86-97.

[31]Richard Christie, "Authoritarianism Re-examined," in Christie and Jahoda, *Scope and Method*, pp. 123-96. See especially pp. 174-5. Kornhauser's findings lead to the same conclusion. See Arthur Kornhauser, Harold L. Sheppard, and Albert J. Mayer, *When Labor Votes* (New York: University Books, 1956), pp. 191-5.

[32]Don Stewart and Thomas Hoult, "A Social-Psychological Theory of the Authoritarian Personality," *American Journal of Sociology 65* (1959): 274-9.

[33] Daniel J. Levinson and Phyllis E. Huffman, "Traditional Family Ideology and Its Relation to Personality," *Journal of Personality 23* (1955): 251-73.

[34]Rotter, et al., "Internal versus External Control."

[35]Frank Barron, "Complexity-Simplicity as a Personality Dimension," *Journal of Abnormal and Social Psychology 48* (1953): 163-72.

[36]Else Frenkel-Brunswik, "Intolerance of Ambiguity as an Emotional and Perceptual Personality Variable," *Journal of Personality 18* (1949): 108-43.

[37]Adorno, et al., *The Authoritarian Personality*, p. 461.

[38]Ibid., p. 467.

[39]Lee Rainwater, Richard P. Coleman, and Gerald Handel, *Workingman's Wife* (New York: Oceana Publications, 1950), p. 59.

[40]Rokeach, "Generalized Mental Rigidity"; Milton Rokeach, " 'Narrow-Mindedness' and Personality," *Journal of Personality 20* (1951-52): 234-51.

[41]Alvin Scodel and Paul Mussen, "Social Perceptions of Authoritarians and Nonauthoritarians," *Journal of Abnormal and Social Psychology 48* (1953): 181-4.

[42]David Riesman, *The Lonely Crowd* (New Haven: Yale University Press, 1961), p. 6.

[43]Ibid., pp. 11-13.

[44]Ibid., pp. 13-17.

[45]Ibid., pp. 19-22.

[46]Ibid., pp. 22-5.

[47]Ibid., p. 17.

[48]Herbert Gans, *The Urban Villagers* (Glencoe, Ill.: Free Press, 1962), pp. 245-6.

[49]Riesman, *The Lonely Crowd*, p. 20.

[50]Ibid., p. 17.

[51]Ibid.

[52]Ibid., p. 18.

[53]Ibid., p. 22.

[54]Ibid., p. 130.

[55]Ibid., p. 81.

[56]Ibid., pp. 71-80.

[57]Ibid., p. 25.

[58]Ibid., p. 82.

[59]Ibid., pp. 16, 246, 259.

[60]Ibid., Chapter III, pp. 66-82.

[61]Ibid., p. 242.

[62]Ibid., p. 259.

[63]Ibid., p. 157.

[64]Ibid., p. 260.

[65]Erik H. Erikson, *Identity: Youth and Crisis* (New York: Norton,

1968), Chapter III, "The Life Cycle: Epigenesis of Identity," pp. 91-141.

[66]Richard M. Jones, *Fantasy and Feeling in Education* (New York: New York University Press, 1968), pp. 130-1.

[67]Ibid., p. 132.

[68]David Elkind, "Erik Erikson's Eight Stages of Man," *New York Times Magazine* (April 5, 1970), pp. 25 ff.

[69]Erikson, *Identity*, Chapter III, pp. 91-141: Elkind, "Eight Stages"; Erik Erikson, *Childhood and Society*, 2nd edition revised and enlarged (New York: Norton, 1963), Chapter 7, "Eight Ages of Man," pp. 219-33.

[70]Harvey, et al., *Conceptual Systems*, pp. 91 and 159 ff.

[71]Gans, *The Urban Villagers*, p. 246. Also note the lower class sex differences in all age groups in Tables VIII and IX (pp. 434 and 435) of Herbert H. Hyman, "The Value Systems of Different Classes: A Social Psychological Contribution to the Analysis of Stratification," in Reinhard Bendix and Seymour M. Lipset (eds.), *Class, Status, and Power* (Glencoe, Ill.: Free Press, 1953), pp. 426-42.

[72]An interesting sidelight on development in lower class children is provided by a study of self-esteem in 3800 children between the ages of eight and thirteen, reported in both of the following: Robert J. Trotter, "Self-Image," *Science News 100* (August 21, 1971): 130-1; Norma Trowbridge, "Effects of Socio-Economic Class on Self-Concept of Children," *Psychology in the Schools 7* (July 1970): 304-6.

An *inverse* relationship was found between social class and self-esteem scores which outweighed differences in age, sex, race, and rural-urban residence. This interesting finding may indicate that the lower class children have experienced an arrest in a progressive personality type and are reflecting in their high level of self-esteem the consolidation and relaxation that accompany closure. The middle class children, by contrast, may be still struggling to improve themselves. The higher the ideal, the more dissatisfaction with the current self. If the lower class children have stalled at a progressive type, it would seem to be Impulsive Action-Seeker (see Table 12). As a result of later experiences, some may progress beyond this to Routine-Seeker or even higher, while others may drop back into an arrestive type (Cynic or Anomic).

Chapter 6

[1]Summarized in Don Martindale, *The Nature and Types of Sociological Theory* (Boston: Houghton Mifflin, 1960), pp. 81-6. For the original, see Ferdinand Toennies, *Community and Society,* translated by Charles P. Loomis (East Lansing, Mich.: Michigan State University Press, 1957).

[2]Summarized in Martindale, *Sociology Theory*, pp. 86-90. For the original see Emile Durkheim, *The Division of Labor in Society*, translated by George Simpson (Glencoe, Ill.: Free Press, 1947).

[3]David Riesman, *The Lonely Crowd* (New Haven: Yale University Press, 1961), pp. 5-7.

[4]Summarized in Martindale, *Sociological Theory,* pp. 383-4, 390-3. For the original, see Hans Gerth and C. Wright Mills (trans. and eds.), *From Max Weber: Essays in Sociology* (New York: Oxford University Press, 1946).

[5]Max Weber, *The Protestant Ethic and the Spirit of Capitalism,* translated by Talcott Parsons (New York: Scribner's, 1958). See especially the author's introduction.

[6]Ibid., pp. 14-5; Martindale, *Sociological Theory,* 383-4; Gerth and Mills, *From Max Weber*, pp. 51-5.

[7]Weber, *The Protestant Ethic,* p. 105. Individualism led to asceticism and to the need to prove by worldly success that one was the recipient of God's grace.

[8]Riesman, *The Lonely Crowd,* pp. 18, 45, 124.

[9]Martindale, *Sociological Theory,* p. 84.

[10]Heinz Werner, *Comparative Psychology of Mental Development* (New York: Harper, 1940), p. 299.

[11]Joseph Church, *Language and the Discovery of Reality* (New York: Random House, 1961), p. 139.

[12]All three are found in Jerome S. Bruner, Rose R. Olver, and Patricia M. Greenfield, *Studies in Cognitive Growth* (New York: Wiley & Sons, 1966): Patricia M. Greenfield, "On Culture and Conservation," pp. 225-56; Michael Maccoby and Nancy Modiano, "On Culture and Equivalence, I," pp. 257-69; Patricia M. Greenfield, Lee C. Reich, and Rose R. Olver, "On Culture and Equivalence, II," pp. 270-318.

[13]Bruner, et al., *Cognitive Growth*, p. 46.

[14]Werner, *Comparative Psychology*, p. 299.

[15]Greenfield, "On Culture and Conservation," p. 226.

[16]Bruner, et al., *Cognitive Growth*, p. 47.

[17]Werner, *Comparative Psychology*, pp. 24-31.

[18]Irving Kristol, "Decentralization for What?" *The Public Interest*, No. 11 (Spring 1968): 17-25; Peter F. Drucker, "The Sickness of Government," *The Public Interest*, No. 14 (Winter 1969): 3-23. Drucker's approach is different. He advocates a stronger, more active government, but one which farms out its programs to private organizations. The state plans and administers only. In doing so, it expands until it is "the" institution overseeing all the rest. Here Drucker seems to suggest that the state expands until its parameters are those of society itself.

[19]Church, *Language*, p. 118.

[20]Robert L. Heilbroner, *The Great Ascent* (New York: Harper & Row Torchbook, 1963), pp. 9 and 84.

[21]O.J. Harvey, David E. Hunt, and Harold M. Schroder, *Conceptual Systems and Personality Organization* (New York: Wiley & Sons, 1961).

[22]Daniel Bell and Mancur Olson, Jr., "Toward a Social Report," *The Public Interest, No. 15* (Spring 1969): 72-105.

[23]The prediction and direction of the future, and the role of social scientists therein, has been much debated. The reports of two recent commissions are most pertinent to the present discussion: that of the American Academy of Arts and Sciences' Commission on the Year 2000, and that of the Special Commission on the Social Sciences of the National Science Board: Daniel Bell (ed.), *Toward the Year 2000: Work in Progress* (Boston: Beacon Press, The Daedalus Library, 1969); National Science Foundation, *Knowledge into Action: Improving the Nation's Use of the Social Sciences* (Washington, D.C.: U. S. Government Printing Office, 1969).

[24]E. Robert LaCrosse, Jr., Patrick C. Lee (ed.), Frances Litman, Daniel M. Ogilvie, Susan S. Stodolsky, and Burton L. White, "The First Six Years of Life: A Report on Current Research and Educational Practice," *Genetic Psychology Monographs 82* (1970): 161-266. See especially p. 255.

[25]Ted Irwin, "How Much Can a Six-Month Infant Learn in School?" *Parade* (January 9, 1972): 10-15.

[26]Ibid., pp. 13, 15.

[27]Ibid., p. 10.

[28]Ibid., p. 15.

[29]James J. Gallagher, "Productive Thinking," in Martin L. and Lois W. Hoffman (eds.), *Review of Child Development Research* (New York: Russell Sage Foundation, 1964), I, pp. 349-381; Samuel Messick, "The Criterion Problem in the Evaluation of Instruction: Assessing Possible, Not Just Probable Intended Outcomes," in M. C. Wittrock and David E. Wiley (eds.), *The Evaluation of Instruction: Issues and Problems* (New York: Holt, Rinehart & Winston, 1970), pp. 188-202. See especially pp. 196-9.

[30]Gallagher, "Productive Thinking," pp. 374-5.

[31]Ibid., pp. 371-2.

[32]Ibid., e.g., the curriculum projects supported by the National Science Foundation in the physical and social sciences.

[33] Claire E. Austin, "The Relationship of Role-Playing and Futuristic Thinking with Ninth Graders," *Journal of Education 152* (April 1970), pp. 11-17; Robert Kastenbaum, "Getting There Ahead of Time," *Psychology Today 5* (December 1971): 52-4, 82-4.

[34] Austin, "Role-Playing"; Martha A. John, "The Relationship of Role-Playing to Futuristic Thinking," *Journal of Education 152* (April 1970): 4-10.

[35]Austin, "Role-Playing."

[36]Urie Bronfenbrenner, *Two Worlds of Childhood: U.S. and U.S.S.R.* (New York: Russell Sage Foundation, 1970), pp. 115-16.

[37]Richard M. Jones, *Fantasy and Feeling in Education* (New York: New York University Press, 1968), p. 160.

[38]Ibid., p. 125. The curriculum was "Man: A Course of Study," developed by the Education Development Center, Inc., of Cambridge, Mass.

[39]Ibid., pp. 191-2. Each of these steps is explained in detail in pp. 192-207.

[40]Ibid., pp. 115, 118-19.

[41]Gallagher, "Productive Thinking," p. 377.

[42]Bronfenbrenner, *Two Worlds*, p. 158. Chapter 6 contains his recommendations on how this can be accomplished.

[43]Ibid., pp. 17-23.

[44]Ibid., pp. 26-69.

[45]Bruno Bettelheim, *The Children of the Dream* (New York: Macmillan, 1969), pp. 71 and 85 ff.

[46]Ibid., pp. 126-9.

[47]Ibid., p. 187.

[48]Arthur G. Neal and Melvin Seeman, "Organizations and Powerlessness: A Test of the Mediation Hypothesis,"*American Sociological Review 29* (1964): 216-26.

[49]William Erbe, "Social Involvement and Political Activity: A Replication and Elaboration," *American Sociological Review 29* (1964): 198-215.

Bibliography

Adams, Bert N. *Kinship in an Urban Setting*. Chicago: Markham, 1968.

Adorno, T. W., Frenkel-Brunswik, Else, Levinson, Daniel J., and Sanford, N. Nevitt. *The Authoritarian Personality*. New York: Harper & Bros., 1950.

Alkire, Armand A. "Social Power and Communication Within Families of Disturbed and Nondisturbed Adolescents," *Journal of Personality and Social Psychology* 13 (1969): 335-349.

Aronfreed, Justin. *Conduct and Conscience*. New York: Academic Press, 1968.

Axelrod, Morris. "Urban Structure and Social Participation," *American Sociological Review* 21 (1956): 13-18.

Baldwin, Alfred L. *Theories of Child Development*. New York: Wiley and Sons, 1968.

Bandura, Albert, and Walters, R. H. *Adolescent Aggression*. New York: Ronald Press, 1959.

Barron, Frank. "Complexity-Simplicity as a Personality Dimension," *Journal of Abnormal and Social Psychology* 48 (1953): 163-172.

Battle, Esther, and Rotter, Julian B. "Children's Feelings of Personal Control as Related to Social Class and Ethnic Group," *Journal of Personality* 31 (1963): 482-490.

Bayley, Nancy, and Schaefer, Earl S. "Relationships Between Socioeconomic Variables and the Behavior of Mothers Toward Young Children," *Journal of Genetic Psychology* 96 (1960): 61-77.

Beardslee, Betty A. J. "The Learning of Two Mechanisms of Defense," *Dissertation Abstracts* 17 (1957): 173-174.

Beilin, Harry. "The Pattern of Postponability and Its Relation to Social Class Mobility," *Journal of Social Psychology* 44 (1956): 33-48.

Bell, Daniel (ed.). *Toward the Year 2000: Work in Progress*. Boston: Beacon Press, The Daedalus Library, 1969.

————, and Olson, Mancur, Jr. "Toward a Social Report," *The Public Interest*, No. 15 (1969): 72-105.

Bell, Wendell. "Anomie, Social Isolation, and Class Structure," *Sociometry* 20 (1957): 105-116.

————, and Force, Maryanne T. "Social Structure and Participation in Different Types of Formal Associations," *Social Forces* 34 (1956): 345-350.

————. "Urban Neighborhood Types and Participation in Formal Associations," *American Sociological Review* 21 (1956): 25-34.

Bendix, Reinhard, and Lipset, Seymour (eds.). *Class, Status, and Power*. Glencoe, Ill.: Free Press, 1953.

Berger, Bennett M. *Working-Class Suburb*. Los Angeles: University of California Press, 1960.

Bernstein, Basil. "Language and Social Class," *British Journal of Sociology* 11 (1960): 271-276.

————. "A Public Language: Some Sociological Implications of a Linguistic Form," *British Journal of Sociology* 10 (1959): 311-326.

————. "Some Sociological Determinants of Perception," *British Journal of Sociology* 9 (1958): 159-174.

Bettelheim, Bruno. *The Children of the Dream*. New York: Macmillan, 1969.

Bialer, Irv. "Conceptualization of Success and Failure in Mentally Retarded and Normal Children," *Journal of Personality* 29 (1961): 303-320.

Bing, Elizabeth. "Effect of Childrearing Practices on Development of Differential Cognitive Abilities," *Child Development* 34 (1963): 631-648.

Blau, Peter M. "Occupational Bias and Mobility," *American Sociological Review* 22 (1957): 392-399.

Blood, Robert O., Jr., and Wolfe, Donald M. *Husbands and Wives*. Glencoe, Ill.: Free Press, 1960.

Bloom, Richard D., Whiteman, Martin, and Deutsch, Martin. "Race and Social Class as Separate Factors," pp. 309-317 in Martin Deutsch and Associates, *The Disadvantaged Child*. New York: Basic Books, 1967.

Boehm, Leonore. "The Development of Conscience: A Comparison of American Children of Different Mental and Socioeconomic Levels," *Child Development* 33 (1962): 575-590.

──────. "The Development of Conscience of Preschool Children: A Cultural and Subcultural Comparison," *Journal of Social Psychology* 59 (1963): 355-360.

──────, and Nass, Martin L. "Social Class Differences in Conscience Development," *Child Development* 33 (1962): 565-574.

Bott, Elizabeth. *Family and Social Network*. London: Tavistock Publications, 1957.

Bronfenbrenner, Urie. "Freudian Theories of Identification and Their Derivatives," pp. 232-254 in Albert D. Ullman (ed.), *Sociocultural Foundations of Personality*. Boston: Houghton Mifflin, 1965.

──────. "Socialization and Social Class Through Time and Space," pp. 400-425 in Eleanor E. Maccoby, Theodore M. Newcomb, and Eugene L. Hartley (eds.), *Readings in Social Psychology*, 3d ed. New York: Holt, Rinehart and Winston, 1958.

──────. "Some Familial Antecedents of Responsibility and Leadership in Adolescents," pp. 239-271 in Luigi Petrullo and Bernard Bass (eds.), *Leadership and Interpersonal Behavior*. New York: Holt, Rinehart and Winston, 1961.

──────. *Two Worlds of Childhood: U.S. and U.S.S.R.* New York: Russell Sage Foundation, 1970.

Cazden, Courtney B. "Subcultural Differences in Child Language: An Interdisciplinary Review," *Merrill-Palmer Quarterly* 12 (1966): 185-219.

Christie, Richard. "Authoritarianism Re-examined," pp. 123-196 in Richard Christie and Marie Jahoda (eds.), *Studies in the Scope and Method of 'The Authoritarian Personality'*. Glencoe, Ill.: Free Press, 1954.

Church, Joseph. *Language and the Discovery of Reality*. New York: Random House, 1961.

Cohen, Albert K., and Hodges, Harold M., Jr. "Characteristics of the Lower-Blue-Collar-Class," *Social Problems* 10 (1963): 303-334.

Conners, C. Keith, Schuette, Corinne, and Goldman, Ann. "Informational Analysis of Intersensory Communication in Children of Different Social Class," *Child Development* 38 (1967): 251-266.

Covington, Martin V. "Stimulus Discrimination as a Function of Social-Class Membership," *Child Development* 38 (1967): 607-613.

Davis, Allison, and Havighurst, Robert J. "Social-Class and Color Differences in Child-Rearing," *American Sociological Review* 11 (1946): 698-710.

Dotson, Floyd. "Patterns of Voluntary Association Among Urban Working Class Families," *American Sociological Review* 16 (1951): 687-693.

Douvan, Elizabeth, and Gold, Martin. "Modal Patterns in American Adolescence," pp. 469-528 in Lois W. Hoffman and Martin L. Hoffman (eds.), *Review of Child Development Research,* II. New York: Russell Sage Foundation, 1966.

Dubin, Robert. "Industrial Workers' Worlds: A Study of the 'Central Life Interests' of Industrial Workers," pp. 247-266 in Arnold M. Rose (ed.), *Human Behavior and Social Process.* Boston: Houghton Mifflin, 1962.

Durkheim, Emile. *The Division of Labor in Society,* translated by George Simpson. Glencoe, Ill.: Free Press, 1947.

Elder, Glen H., Jr. "Structural Variations in the Child Rearing Relationship," *Sociometry* 25 (1962): 241-262.

———, and Bowerman, Charles E. "Family Structure and Child-Rearing Patterns: The Effect of Family Size and Sex Composition," *American Sociological Review* 28 (1963): 891-905.

Elkind, David, Koegler, Ronald R., and Go, Elsie. "Field Independence and Concept Formation," *Perceptual and Motor Skills* 17 (1963): 383-386.

Erbe, William. "Social Involvement and Political Activity: A Replication and Elaboration," *American Sociological Review* 29 (1964): 198-215.

Erikson, Eric H. *Childhood and Society,* 2d ed. New York: Norton, 1963.

———. *Identity: Youth and Crisis.* New York: Norton, 1968.

Feffer, Melvin H. "Cognitive Aspects of Role-Taking in Children," *Journal of Personality* 28 (1960): 383-396.

———. "The Cognitive Implications of Role-Taking Behavior," *Journal of Personality* 27 (1959): 152-168.

Findlay, Donald C., and McGuire, Carson. "Social Status and Abstract Behavior," *Journal of Abnormal and Social Psychology* 54 (1957): 135-137.

Flavell, John H. *The Developmental Psychology of Jean Piaget*. Princeton, N. J.: Van Nostrand, 1963.

Ford, Julienne, Young, Douglas, and Box, Steven. "Functional Autonomy, Role Distance, and Social Class," *British Journal of Sociology* 18 (1967): 370-381.

Gallagher, James J. "Productive Thinking," pp. 349-381 in Martin L. Hoffman and Lois W. Hoffman (eds.), *Review of Child Development Research*, I. New York: Russell Sage Foundation, 1964.

Gans, Herbert. *The Urban Villagers*. Glencoe, Ill.: Free Press, 1962.

Gerth, Hans, and Mills, C. Wright (trans. and eds.). *From Max Weber: Essays in Sociology*. New York: Oxford University Press, 1946.

Glidewell, John C., Kantor, Mildred B., Smith, Louis M., and Stringer, Lorene A. "Socialization and Social Structure in the Classroom," pp. 221-256 in Lois W. Hoffman and Martin L. Hoffman (eds.), *Review of Child Development Research*, II. New York: Russell Sage Foundation, 1966.

Gollin, Eugene S. "Organizational Characteristics of Social Judgment: A Developmental Investigation," *Journal Of Personality* 26 (1958): 139-154.

Gordon, Milton. *Social Class in American Sociology*. Durham, N.C.: Duke University Press, 1958.

Gore, Pearl, and Rotter, Julian B. "A Personality Correlate of Social Action," *Journal of Personality* 31 (1963): 58-64.

Gourevitch, Vivian, and Feffer, Melvin H. "A Study of Motivational Development," *Journal of Genetic Psychology* 100 (1962): 361-375.

Graves, Theodore D. "Time Perspective and the Deferred Gratification Pattern in a Tri-Ethnic Community," Research Report #5, Tri-Ethnic Research Project. Boulder: University of Colorado, 1961.

Greenfield, Patricia M. "On Culture and Conservation," pp. 225-256 in Jerome S. Bruner, Rose R. Olver, and Patricia M. Greenfield (eds.), *Studies in Cognitive Growth*. New York: Wiley and Sons, 1966.

————, Reich, Lee C., and Olver, Rose R. "On Culture and Equivalence, II," pp. 270-318 in Bruner, Olver, and Greenfield, *Studies in Cognitive Growth*. New York: Wiley and Sons, 1966.

Handel, Gerald, and Rainwater, Lee. "Persistence and Change in Working Class Life Style." Unpublished paper. Chicago: Social Research, Inc., 1963.

Harvey, O. J., Hunt, David E., and Schroder, Harold M. *Conceptual Systems and Personality Organization*. New York: Wiley and Sons, 1961.

Havighurst, Robert J., and Davis, Allison, "A Comparison of the Chicago and Harvard Studies of Social Class Differences in Child-Rearing," *American Sociological Review* 20 (1955): 438-442.

Heber, Rick F., and Dever, Richard B. "Research on Education and Habilitation of the Mentally Retarded," pp. 395-427 in H. Carl Haywood (ed.), *Social-Cultural Aspects of Mental Retardation*. New York: Meredith Corporation of Appleton-Century-Crofts, 1970.

Hess, Robert D. "Educability and Rehabilitation: The Future of the Welfare Class," *Journal of Marriage and the Family* 26 (1964): 422-429.

————, and Shipman, Virginia C. "Early Experience and the Socialization of Cognitive Modes in Children," *Child Development* 36 (1965): 869-886.

Hoffman, Martin L. "Childrearing Practices and Moral Development: Generalizations from Empirical Research," *Child Development* 34 (1963): 295-318.

————. "Parent Discipline and the Child's Consideration for Others," *Child Development* 34 (1963): 573-588.

————. "Power Assertion by the Parent and Its Impact on the Child," *Child Development* 31 (1960): 129-143.

————, and Saltzstein, Herbert D. "Parent Discipline and the Child's Moral Development," *Journal of Personality and Social Psychology* 5 (1967): 45-57.

Hoggart, Richard. *The Uses of Literacy*. London: Chatto and Windus, 1959.

Hollingshead, August, and Redlich, Frederick C. *Social Class and Mental Illness*. New York: Wiley and Sons, 1958.

Hunt, David E., and Dopyera, John. "Personality Variation in Lower-Class Children," *Journal of Psychology* 62 (1966): 47-54.

John, Vera P. "The Intellectual Development of Slum Children: Some Preliminary Findings," *American Journal of Orthopsychiatry* 33 (1963): 813-822.

Jones, Richard M. *Fantasy and Feeling in Education*. New York: New York University Press, 1968.

Judson, Abe J., and Tuttle, Cynthia E. "Time Perspective and Social Class," *Perceptual and Motor Skills* 23 (1966): 1074.

Kagan, Jerome. "Reflection-Impulsivity and Reading Ability in Primary Grade Children," *Child Development* 36 (1965): 609-628.

———, Pearson, Leslie, and Welch, Lois. "Conceptual Impulsivity and Inductive Reasoning," *Child Development* 37 (1966): 583-594.

Kahl, Joseph, and Davis, James A. "A Comparison of Indexes of Socioeconomic Status," *American Sociological Review* 20 (1955): 317-325.

Kamii, Constance K., and Radin, Norma L. "Class Differences in the Socialization Practices of Negro Mothers," *Journal of Marriage and the Family* 29 (1967): 302-310.

Kantor, Mildred B., Glidewell, John D., Mensh, Ivan N., Domke, Herbert R., and Gildea, Margaret. "Socio-Economic Level and Maternal Attitudes Toward Parent-Child Relationships," *Human Organization* 16 (1958): 44-48.

Kohlberg, Lawrence. "Development of Moral Character and Moral Ideology," pp. 383-431 in Martin L. Hoffman and Lois W. Hoffman (eds.), *Review of Child Development Research*, I. New York: Russell Sage Foundation, 1964.

Kohn, Melvin L. "Social Class and the Exercise of Parental Authority," *American Sociological Review* 24 (1959): 352-366.

———. "Social Class and Parental Values," *American Journal of Sociology* 64 (1959): 337-351.

———. "Social Class and Parent-Child Relationships: An Interpretation," *American Journal of Sociology* 68 (1963): 471-480.

———, and Carroll, Eleanor E. "Social Class and the Allocation of Parental Responsibilities," *Sociometry* 23 (1960): 372-392.

———, and Schooler, Carmi. "Class, Occupation, and Orientation," *American Sociological Review* 34 (1969): 659-678.

Komarovsky, Mirra. "The Voluntary Associations of Urban Dwellers," *American Sociological Review* 11 (1946): 686-698.

Kornhauser, Arthur, Sheppard, Harold L., and Mayer, Albert J. *When Labor Votes*. New York: University Books, 1956.

Kristol, Irving. "Decentralization for What?" *The Public Interest,* No. 11 (1968): 17-25.

LaCrosse, E. Robert, Jr., Lee, Patrick C., (ed.), Litman, Frances, Ogilvie, Daniel M., Stodolsky, Susan S., and White, Burton L. "The First Six Years of Life: A Report on Current Research and Educational Practice," *Genetic Psychology Monographs* 82 (1970): 161-266.

Lasswell, Thomas E. *Class and Stratum*. Boston: Houghton Mifflin, 1965.

Lehmann, Irving J. "Some Socio-Cultural Differences in Attitudes and Values," *Journal of Educational Sociology* 36 (1962): 1-9.

LeShan, Lawrence L. "Time Orientation and Social Class," *Journal of Abnormal and Social Psychology* 47 (1952): 589-592.

Levinson, Daniel J., and Huffman, Phyllis E. "Traditional Family Ideology and Its Relation to Personality," *Journal of Personality* 23 (1955): 251-273.

Lipset, Seymour, M. *Political Man*. Garden City, N. Y.: Doubleday, 1960.

————. "Working-Class Authoritarianism," pp. 527-557 in Bartlett H. Stoodley (ed.), *Society and Self*. Glencoe, Ill.: Free Press, 1962.

————, and Bendix, Reinhard. *Social Mobility in Industrial Society*. Berkeley and Los Angeles: University of California Press, 1959.

Littman, Richard A., Moore, Robert C. A., and Pierce-Jones, John. "Social Class Differences in Child Rearing: A Third Community for Comparison With Chicago and Newton," *American Sociological Review* 22 (1957): 694-704.

Maas, Henry. "Some Social Class Differences in the Family Systems and Group Relations of Pre- and Early Adolescents," *Child Development* 22 (1951): 145-152.

Maccoby, Michael, and Modiano, Nancy. "On Culture and Equivalence, I," pp. 257-269 in Bruner, Olver, and Greenfield, *Studies in Cognitive Growth*. New York: Wiley and Sons, 1966.

MacRae, Duncan, Jr. "A Test of Piaget's Theories of Moral Development," *Journal of Abnormal and Social Psychology* 49 (1954): 14-18.

Maier, Henry W. *Three Theories of Child Development.* New York: Harper, Row, 1965.

Martindale, Don. *The Nature and Types of Sociological Theory.* Boston: Houghton Mifflin, 1960.

Massari, David, Hayweiser, Lois, and Meyer, William J. "Activity Level and Intellectual Functioning in Deprived Preschool Children," *Developmental Psychology* 1 (1969): 286-290.

Mayer, Kurt B., and Buckley, Walter. *Class and Society.* New York: Random House, 1970.

McCarthy, Dorothea. "Language Development in the Child," pp. 492-630 in Leonard Carmichael (ed.), *Manual of Child Psychology*, 2d ed. New York: Wiley and Sons, 1954.

McGrade, Betty Jo. "Effectiveness of Verbal Reinforcers in Relation to Age and Social Class," *Journal of Personality and Social Psychology* 4 (1966): 555-560.

McGuire, Carson. "Family Life in Lower and Middle Class Homes," *Marriage and Family Living* 14 (1952): 1-6.

McNeil, Elton B. "Conceptual and Motoric Expressiveness in Two Social Classes," *Dissertation Abstracts* 13 (1953): 437.

Messick, Samuel. "The Criterion Problem in the Evaluation of Instruction: Assessing Possible, Not Just Probable Intended Outcomes," pp. 188-202 in M. C. Wittrock and David E. Wiley (eds.), *The Evaluation of Instruction: Issues and Problems.* New York: Holt, Rinehart and Winston, 1970.

Milgram, Norman, and Goodglass, Harold. "Role Style versus Cognitive Maturation in Word Associations of Adults and Children," *Journal of Personality* 29 (1961): 81-93.

Miller, Daniel R., and Swanson, Guy E. *Inner Conflict and Defense.* New York: Henry Holt, 1960.

Miller, S. M. "The American Lower Classes: A Typological Approach." Unpublished paper. Syracuse, N. Y.: Syracuse University Youth Development Center, 1963.

————, and Riessman, Frank. " 'Working-class Authoritarianism': A Critique of Lipset," *British Journal of Sociology* 12 (1961): 263-276.

————. "The Working Class Subculture: A New View," *Social Problems* 9 (1961): 86-97.

Miller, Walter B. "Implications of Urban Lower-Class Culture for Social Work," *Social Service Review* 33 (1959): 219-236.

————. "Lower Class Culture as a Generating Milieu of Gang Delinquency," *Journal of Social Issues* 14 (1958): 5-19.

Misch, Robert C. "The Relationship of Motoric Inhibition to Developmental Level and Ideational Functioning: An Analysis by Means of the Rorschach Test," *Dissertation Abstracts* 14 (1954): 1810-1811.

Mizruchi, Ephraim H. "Social Structure and Anomia in a Small City," *American Sociological Review* 25 (1960): 644-654.

Morse, Nancy C., and Weiss, Robert S. "The Function and Meaning of Work and the Job," *American Sociological Review* 20 (1955): 191-198.

Moss, Howard A., Robson, Kenneth S., and Pedersen, Frank. "Determinants of Maternal Stimulation of Infants and Consequences of Treatment for Later Reactions to Strangers," *Developmental Psychology* 1 (1969): 239-246.

Myers, Jerome, and Roberts, Bertram. *Family and Class Dynamics in Mental Illness*. New York: Wiley and Sons, 1959.

National Science Foundation. *Knowledge Into Action: Improving the Nation's Use of the Social Sciences*. Washington, D. C.: U. S. Government Printing Office, 1969.

Neal, Arthur G., and Seeman, Melvin. "Organizations and Powerlessness: A Test of the Mediation Hypothesis," *American Sociological Review* 29 (1964): 216-226.

Olsen, Marvin E. "Social Participation and Voting Turnout: A Multivariate Analysis," *American Sociological Review* 37 (1972): 317-333.

Pease, John, Form, William H., and Rytina, Joan Huber. "Ideological Currents in American Stratification Literature," *American Sociologist* 5 (1970): 127-137.

Peck, Robert F., and Havighurst, Robert J. *The Psychology of Character Development*. New York: Wiley and Sons, 1960.

Pfautz, Harold W. "The Current Literature on Social Stratification, Critique and Bibliography," *American Journal of Sociology* 58 (1953): 391-418.

Piaget, Jean. *The Moral Judgment of the Child*. Glencoe, Ill.: Free Press, 1932.

Rainwater, Lee. *And the Poor Get Children*. Chicago: Quadrangle Books, 1960.

———. "Marital Sexuality in Four Cultures of Poverty," *Journal of Marriage and the Family* 26 (1964): 457-466.

———, Coleman, Richard P., and Handel, Gerald. *Workingman's Wife*. New York: Oceana Publications, 1950.

———, and Handel, Gerald. "Changing Family Roles in the Working Class." Unpublished paper. Chicago: Social Research, Inc. 1963.

Reissman, Leonard. "Class, Leisure, and Social Participation," *American Sociological Review* 19 (1954): 76-84.

Riesman, David. *The Lonely Crowd*. New Haven: Yale University Press, 1961.

Riessman, Frank. *The Culturally Deprived Child*. New York: Harper, Row, 1962.

Rodman, Hyman, "The Lower Class Value Stretch," *Social Forces* 42 (1963): 205-215.

Rokeach, Milton. "Generalized Mental Rigidity as a Factor in Ethnocentrism," *Journal of Abnormal and Social Psychology* 43 (1948): 259-278.

———. " 'Narrow-Mindedness' and Personality," *Journal of Personality* 20 (1951-1952): 234-251.

———. "Prejudice, Concreteness of Thinking, and Reification of Thinking," *Journal of Abnormal and Social Psychology* 46 (1951): 83-91.

Rosengren, William R. "Social Status, Attitudes Toward Pregnancy and Child-Rearing Attitudes," *Social Forces* 41 (1962): 127-134.

Rotter, Julian B. "Generalized Expectancies for Internal versus External Control of Reinforcements," *Psychological Monographs* 80, Monograph 609 (1966).

———, Seeman, Melvin, and Liverant, Shephard. "Internal versus External Control of Reinforcements: A Major Variable in Behavior Theory," pp. 473-516 in Norman F. Washburne (ed.), *Decisions, Values and Groups*, II. London: Pergamon Press, 1962.

Salzinger, Suzanne, Salzinger, Kurt, and Hobson, Sally. "The Effect of Syntactical Structure on Immediate Memory for Word Sequences in

Middle- and Lower-Class Children," *Journal of Psychology* 67 (1967): 147-159.

Schatzman, Leonard, and Strauss, Anselm. "Social Class and Modes of Communication," *American Journal of Sociology* 60 (1955): 329-338.

Schneider, Louis, and Lysgaard, Sverre. "The Deferred Gratification Pattern: A Preliminary Study," *American Sociological Review* 18 (1953): 142-149.

Schwebel, Andrew I. "Effects of Impulsivity on Performance of Verbal Tasks in Middle- and Lower-Class Children," *American Journal of Orthopsychiatry* 36 (1966): 13-21.

Scodel, Alvin, and Mussen, Paul. "Social Perceptions of Authoritarians and Nonauthoritarians," *Journal of Abnormal and Social Psychology* 48 (1953): 181-184.

Sears, Robert R., Maccoby, Eleanor, and Levin, Harry. *Patterns of Child Rearing*. Evanston, Ill.: Row, Peterson, 1957.

Shostak, Arthur B., and Gomberg, William (eds.). *Blue-Collar World*. Englewood Cliffs, N. J. : Prentice-Hall, 1964.

Siller, Jerome. "Socioeconomic Status and Conceptual Thinking," *Journal of Abnormal and Social Psychology* 55 (1957): 365-371.

Smart, Susan. "Social Class Differences in Parent Behavior in a Natural Setting," *Journal of Marriage and the Family* 26 (1964): 223-224.

Spinley, Betty M. *The Deprived and the Privileged*. London: Routledge and Kegan Paul, 1953.

Stewart, Don, and Hoult, Thomas. "A Social-Psychological Theory of the Authoritarian Personality," *American Journal of Sociology* 65 (1959): 274-279.

Stodolsky, Susan, and Lesser, Gerald S. "Learning Patterns in the Disadvantaged," pp. 168-177 in Marcel L. Goldschmid (ed.), *Black Americans and White Racism*. New York: Holt, Rinehart and Winston, 1970.

Stoltz, Robert E., and Smith, Marshall D. "Some Effects of Socio-Economic, Age and Sex Factors on Children's Responses to the Rosenzweig Picture-Frustration Study," *Journal of Clinical Psychology* 15 (1959): 200-203.

Straus, Murray A. "Communication, Creativity, and Problem-Solving Ability of Middle- and Working-Class Families in Three

Societies," *American Journal of Sociology* 73 (1968): 417-430.
———. "Deferred Gratification, Social Class, and the Achievement Syndrome," *American Sociological Review* 27 (1962): 326-335.

Sussman, Marvin B. "The Isolated Nuclear Family: Fact or Fiction," *Social Problems* 6 (1959): 333-340.

Terrell, Glenn, Jr., and Durkin, Kathryn. "Social Class and the Nature of the Incentive in Discrimination Learning," *Journal of Abnormal and Social Psychology* 59 (1959): 270-272.

Toennies, Ferdinand. *Community and Society*, translated by Charles P. Loomis. East Lansing, Mich.: Michigan State University Press, 1957.

Trowbridge, Norma. "Effects of Socio-Economic Class on Self- Concept of Children," *Psychology in the Schools* 7 (1970): 304-306.

Tuma, Elias, and Livson, Norman. "Family Socioeconomic Status and Adolescent Attitudes Toward Authority," *Child Development* 31 (1960): 387-399.

Turiel, Elliot. "An Experimental Test of the Sequentiality of Developmental Stages in the Child's Moral Judgments," *Journal of Personality and Social Psychology* 3 (1966): 611-618.

Udry, J. Richard. "Marital Instability by Race, Sex, Education, and Occupation Using 1960 Census Data," *American Journal of Sociology* 72 (1967): 203-209.

Ullman, Albert D. "Identification: An Interactionist Interpretation." Unpublished paper. Medford, Mass.: Tufts University, 1954.

Wallace, Melvin, and Rabin, Albert I. "Temporal Experience," *Psychological Bulletin* 57 (1960): 213-236.

Walters, James, Connor, Ruth, and Zunich, Michael. "Interaction of Mothers and Children from Lower-Class Families," *Child Development* 35 (1964): 433-440.

Warner, W. Lloyd, Low, J. O., Lunt, Paul S., and Srole, Leo. *Yankee City*. Abridged ed. New Haven: Yale University Press, 1963.

Weber, Max. *The Protestant Ethic and the Spirit of Capitalism*, translated by Talcott Parsons. New York: Scribner's 1958.

Weinstock, Allen R. "Longitudinal Study of Social Class and Defense Preferences," *Journal of Consulting Psychology* 31 (1967): 539-541.

Werner, Heinz. "The Concept of Development from a Comparative and

Organismic Point of View," pp. 125-148 in Dale B. Harris (ed.), *The Concept of Development*. Minneapolis: University of Minnesota Press, 1957.

White, Burton L., et al. *Experience and Environment: Major Influences on the Development of the Young Child*. Englewoods Cliffs, N. J.: Prentice-Hall, 1973.

Wilensky, Harold L. "Class, Class Consciousness, and American Workers," pp. 423-437 in Maurice Zeitlin (ed.), *American Society, Inc.* Chicago: Markham, 1970.

Williams, Judith R., and Scott, Roland B. "Growth and Development of Negro Infants: IV. Motor Development and its Relationship to Child Rearing Practices in Two Groups of Negro Infants," *Child Development* 24 (1953): 103-121.

Williams, Robin H., Jr. *American Society*. New York: Knopf, 1959.

Witkin, H. A., Lewis, H. B., Hertzman, M., Machover, K., Meissner, P. Bretnall, and Wapman, S. *Personality Through Perception*. New York: Harper, 1954.

Wolfe, Raymond. "The Role of Conceptual Systems in Cognitive Functioning at Varying Levels of Age and Intelligence, *Journal of Personality* 31 (1963): 108-123.

Wright, Charles R., and Hyman, Herbert H. "Voluntary Association Memberships of American Adults: Evidence from National Surveys," *American Sociological Review* 23 (1958): 284-294.

Young, Harl H. "A Test of Witkin's Field-Dependence Hypothesis," *Journal of Abnormal and Social Psychology* 59 (1959): 188-192.

Zigler, Edward. "Social Class and the Socialization Process," *Review of Educational Research* 40 (1970): 87-110.

———, and Child, Irvin L. "Intrasocietal Variation in Socialization," pp. 583-601 in Gardner Lindzey and Elliot Aronson (eds.), *The Handbook of Social Psychology*, 2d ed., III. Reading, Mass.: Addison-Wesley, 1969.

———, and Kanzer, Paul. "The Effectiveness of Two Classes of Verbal Reinforcers on the Performance of Middle- and Lower-Class Children," *Journal of Personality* 30 (1962): 157-163.

Zweig, Ferdynand. *The Worker in an Affluent Society*. Glencoe, Ill.: Free Press, 1961.

Index

(Numbers in italics indicate pages
upon which tables or figures
occur.)

Activity. *See* Middle class, value
    system
  cognitive development and, 109
  Erikson's types and, 138, 148
  interaction patterns and, 103
  linguistic style and, 57
  moral development and, 83
  primary, group style and, 98
  Riesman's types and, 126,
    137-8
Adorno, T. W., 118-123, *134-5*
Affective or moral development
  activity and, 83
  Adorno's stages of development
    and, 118-21
  child-rearing or disciplinary
    style and, 34-8, 80-1, 119-21
  cognitive development and,
    22-3, 31 f., 59, 107, 118,
    121-3, 176-7
  day care programs and, 173-4,
    178-9, 181
  definition of, 59
  effect of parents' developmental
    level on, 59, 65, 71, 82
  Erikson's stages of development

    and, 132-42, 143, *144-5*,
    146, 150
  external-internal control and,
    63-4, 66-8, 70-4, 78-82
  identification and, 60-3, 65, 82
  passivity and, 68, 82
  rationalism and, 65, 79-81
  role-taking ability and, 52,
    63-4, 66
  school system and, 177-80,
    184-6
  sex differences in, 61-3, 66-8,
    82
  social change or planning and,
    168-9, 173, 177-80, 184-6
  social class position and, 59-83
  stimulus-bondage and, 118
  See also Conscience
Aronfreed, Justin, 73-4
Authoritarianism
  child-rearing and, 37, 67,
    119-21
  cognitive style and, 118-21
  component factors of, 118-9
  concreteness and, 118-9, 122-3
  "concretistic personality" and,
    122-3
  conscience development and,
    120
  developmental aspects of,